MW01032051

UFOs and the Alien Presence
Six Viewpoints

Edited and with an Introduction by
Michael Lindemann

Wild Flower Press
P.O. Box 726
Newberg, Oregon 97132

Publisher's Cataloging-in-Publication Data

Lindemann, Michael, 1949-
UFOs and the alien presence: six viewpoints / edited and with an
      introduction by Michael Lindemann.
     p.   cm.

Originally published: Santa Barbara, Calif. : 2020 Group. 1991.
      Contents: The case for UFOs as alien spacecraft and the government
UFO cover-up / Stanton Friedman — The "alien harvest" and beyond /
Linda Moulton Howe — Alien technology in government hands / Bob
Lazar — The case for abduction / Budd Hopkins — Personal encounters /
"Tom" — The "larger reality" behind UFOs / Donald M. Ware.

Included bibliographical references.
      ISBN: 0-926524-08-9
1. Unidentified flying objects   I. Lindemann, Michael.

[TL789.U22   1995]   95-16920
001.9'42--dc20   CIP

Manufactured in the USA
The 2020 Group
          First printing: July 1991
          Third printing: March 1993

Wild Flower Press
          Fourth printing: May 1995

UFOs AND THE ALIEN PRESENCE
SIX VIEWPOINTS

Table of Contents:

Contents, cont'd

Acknowledgments

This book could not have been written without the contributions of many people. Thanks go above all to the six people — Stanton Friedman, Linda Howe, Budd Hopkins, Bob Lazar, Don Ware and Tom — whose interviews comprise the book's six chapters. All of them were totally cooperative throughout the long process that turns raw interviews into final text. They all checked their edited interviews for accuracy, provided photos and background information, answered numerous extra questions, and in general displayed patience and good will at every turn. I am deeply grateful to each one of them.

Thanks goes next to my research associate, Ralph Steiner. Ralph is an award-winning radio producer who resides in Berkeley, California. He conducted the interviews with Stan Friedman and Linda Howe that appear in this book, and joined me in interviewing Bob Lazar. Ralph and I work together on UFO-related investigations, sharing all our sources and data; he as a radio journalist, I as a print journalist. He has made my work on this book much easier.

Thanks to Gene Huff for special assistance on the Bob Lazar interview. Thanks also to Vicki Cooper and Don Ecker at *UFO* magazine; and to Bill Hamilton, Fred Beckman, Jacques Vallee, William L. Moore, David at CUFOS, Shawn Atlanti, Charles Hickson, Bob Girard and Don Berliner.

Thanks to Crit Taylor and Karen Thomas for the cover artwork. Thanks to Steve Diamond, Peter Lindemann and Terri Newlon for encouragement and good ideas. Thanks to Leslie for everything.

Finally, a special note of thanks to those who have requested anonymity, without whose help the truth of the alien presence might never be known. — ML

UFOs and the Alien Presence
Six Viewpoints

The fact is, the information simply can't be kept under wraps any more. It's just bursting out at the seams. And I think our little friends from the sky, whoever they are, are aiding and abetting this slow consciousness-raising that's taking place, for the public to accept that these things are real.

— Budd Hopkins

Introduction

Unexpected events can signal the onset of huge changes in human affairs. One such event took place on the night of July 2, 1947, on a ranch not far from Roswell, New Mexico.

Something strange fell from the stormy sky that night, leaving a trail of wreckage hundreds of feet wide and three-quarters of a mile long. The wreckage was discovered the next morning by ranch manager Mac Brazel, who brought it to the attention of military authorities at Roswell Army Air Force Base. After an initial examination of materials from the crash site, the base commander declared in a press release that a "flying disk" of unknown origin had been recovered. The announcement was an instant sensation. "RAAF Captures Flying Saucer" headlined the Roswell *Daily Record* of July 8.

However, one day later, commanding General Roger Ramey at Carswell Army Air Force Base in Texas officially declared the first report to be in error. Evidently acting on direct orders from Washington, Ramey said that the alleged "flying disk" had turned out to be just a weather balloon. Apologies were made, witnesses declined further comment, and the "weather balloon" was secretly flown to Wright Field (now Wright-Patterson Air Force Base) in Dayton, Ohio, never to be seen again. Thus was a potentially earth-shaking story consigned to oblivion, where it rested for over 30 years.

Today, thanks to the determined efforts of UFO researchers, the so-called Roswell incident is recognized as a milestone in the unfolding drama of human-alien contact on planet earth. That a majority of Americans, along with most people the world over, still remain uninformed about this incident testifies to the power and ingenuity of official efforts to keep it secret. Yet, the evidence supporting claims that the "weather balloon" was, after all, a flying object of unknown origin is now so voluminous as to virtually rule out contrary explanations.

What crashed in 1947 near Roswell did signal a turning point in history, for it made plain the fact that non-human intelligence, equipped with astounding technology, was present on the earth.

Waking up to this fact can be an unsettling development in one's life. For me, this development began in August of 1989, when I first took a serious look at evidence pertaining to UFOs and the alleged alien presence. On recognizing that I could not casually brush this evidence aside, I felt almost unable to function. I sensed that if claims of the alien presence were even partly true, they must eventually come to bear upon every dimension of human affairs. After regaining my composure, I decided to learn all I could about the subject and found its importance growing clearer with every passing day. In December of 1989, I launched the Visitors Investigation Project as a special focus of my future-studies organization, the 2020 Group; and in March of 1990, I published a brief summary of initial findings titled *UFOs and the Alien Presence: Time for the Truth*.

An unexpected outcome of this modest first effort was that I soon found myself talking with many of the most accomplished UFO researchers in America. Some of these people have pursued the maddeningly elusive evidence of the alien presence for decades, and their willingness to share their hard-won understandings with me face to face has accelerated my own learning as nothing else could.

This brings me to the purpose of the present book. During 1990, several of these researchers consented to in-depth interviews with me and my associate Ralph Steiner. These interviews trace the paths these researchers have followed in coming to their present viewpoints on the alien presence. Each one, therefore, is a personal story of the quest to find meaning and order in a body of data that is often shocking in its implications, yet also frustrating in its incompleteness. These interviews, supported by numerous annotations, form the body of this book. My hope is that this approach will make the subject of the alien presence more accessible and compelling to a general audience.

Toward the end of his life, the noted astronomer and UFO researcher J. Allen Hynek said, "We don't have UFOs, only UFO reports." At first glance, this statement might seem to reduce the phenomenon to a collection of wild stories, signifying no more than the all-too-human penchant for self-deception and wishful thinking. But Hynek made clear that this was not his intent. He was acknowledging that, at present, there is nowhere that the interested citizen can go for incontrovertible evidence of the alien presence. No public museum houses alien artifacts. No craft of unknown origin has ever landed on the White House lawn for the benefit of television news. Not one UFO photo out of thousands has yet been accorded the status of absolute authenticity. Lacking such things as would silence skepticism once and for all, researchers must admit that the argument for an alien presence on earth rests mainly upon a huge number of reports from witnesses who are, or ought to be, inherently credible. These witnesses include police officers, airline pilots, military personnel, highly educated professionals of many kinds, and tens of thousands of citizens from all walks of life who risk great discomfort, with little hope of personal gain, in telling their frequently bizarre stories of alien visitation. Far from belittling these "mere" reports, Hynek insisted that their volume and consistency demanded serious scientific attention.

There is other evidence, to be sure. Though every known UFO photo to date is subject to various criticisms, some have been studied by expert photo analysts and judged likely to be authentic. Though the phenomenon of alien abduction is evidenced mainly in the stories told by alleged abductees, it is supported by inexplicable physical scars and undeniable psychological trauma in many cases. Then there are the physical traces allegedly left by alien craft, including burn rings, odd concentrations of radiation, changes in soil chemistry and compaction, and so forth. Over 4,000 such trace cases have been compiled around the world by UFO researchers. Other "traces" include mysterious animal mutilations and crop circles. In recent years, there has been growing speculation that neither of these widespread and highly visible phenomena can be explained without reference to alien activity.

And what of alleged top-secret documents that have recently come to light, purporting to describe the U.S. government's long-time covert handling of the alien presence? Chief among these are the so-called MJ-12 documents, first brought to public attention in 1987. As recounted by former *New York Times* journalist Howard Blum in his 1990 book *Out There*, the FBI launched a top-priority investigation of the MJ-12 documents in order to determine whether they were authentic and, if so, who was responsible for their release, which would constitute an act of espionage. To their evident embarrassment, Blum says, they could not answer either question.

The investigative approach to such documents is always to prove fraud, if possible, since proving authenticity is much more difficult. But regarding MJ-12, the FBI could not prove fraud (much as they might have wanted to). Alongside that, as recounted in the present book, UFO researcher Stanton Friedman did an exhaustive analysis of these documents, also looking for signs of fraud. In his opinion, there are none. Indeed, many small details argue strongly *against* the possibility of fraud. If, therefore, we regard these documents as probably authentic, we are left to conclude that the alien presence is not only abundantly real but also the best-kept secret in history. If, on the other hand, the documents represent a fraud of such exceptional quality that neither the FBI nor other expert investigators can detect it, we are most probably dealing with officially-contrived disinformation on a level rarely seen before. And we must ask why.

Taken all together, the evidence for an alien presence on earth is enormous. Few people on earth know that evidence better, or have thought about it more carefully, than the researchers who speak in the following pages:

Stanton Friedman, a nuclear physicist whose long scientific career spans both private industry and classified government projects, has investigated UFOs for some three decades.

He is probably the top independent authority on the U.S. government's UFO cover-up, as well as a firm advocate of the proposition that at least some UFOs are bona fide alien spacecraft of extraterrestrial origin.

Linda Moulton Howe, a documentary film-maker whose production credits include work for CNN and the Fox television network, has become the outstanding expert on animal mutilation and its probable origins in alien activity since her award-winning documentary *A Strange Harvest* was released in 1980.

Budd Hopkins, a successful New York artist, is largely responsible for bringing the phenomenon of abduction to the forefront of current UFO research with his publication of two best-selling books on the subject during the past decade. Recently, he has established the Intruders Foundation to accommodate the growing demand for assistance from traumatized abductees.

Donald Ware, a career Air Force officer schooled in nuclear engineering, has studied the UFO phenomenon for some three decades and today is Eastern Regional Director for the Mutual UFO Network. Don played a key role in MUFON's investigation of the now-famous Gulf Breeze UFO sightings. Recently, he has turned his attention to what he calls "the larger reality" behind UFOs, contending that the main intent of the alien presence is to help usher in a new spiritual dimension to human existence.

Alongside these four accomplished researchers, I have included in this book two other people whose personal stories serve to illustrate the profound complexity of alleged human-alien interaction.

The first of these people is already famous in UFO circles. His name is Bob Lazar, and he claims to have been hired by the Office of Naval Intelligence to conduct engineering studies of an operational alien spacecraft at a secret government base in Nevada. Bob has become the subject of endless speculation among pundits of every stripe. The bottom-line question, of course, is simply this: Is he telling the truth? In this book, he recounts his story more fully than ever before. Having sat eyeball to eyeball with him as he spoke, having considered the efforts of those who purport to discredit him, and having recently heard from new witnesses whose claims parallel Lazar's in many respects, I offer my own opinion: I think he is telling the truth. If I'm right, his testimony has devastating implications.

The other personal story in this book is told by "Tom," a successful businessman living in Santa Barbara, California. In a sense, Tom's story represents the untold stories of thousands of ordinary citizens who, unknown to their friends and associates, harbor a deep secret: they have encountered the alien presence, not once but many times, and it has indelibly marked their lives.

It seems only fair to acknowledge that many other people could have been invited to speak in the pages of a book like this, circumstances permitting. There are, at a conservative guess, at least several dozen researchers in the United States alone whose expertise and contributions to our knowledge of the UFO phenomenon rival those of the people presented here. There are, furthermore, at least as many also working in Europe, Latin America and other parts of the world. I for one feel indebted to them all.

I also feel obliged to say that this book makes no attempt to represent a true cross-section of opinion on the alien presence. Such a cross-section would include at least the following four categories of opinion.

First, there are substantial numbers of well-informed people who insist that all UFOs and alleged close encounters can be explained as natural phenomena or, in some cases, the products of human folly or fraud. It is certainly true that many UFO sightings can be attributed to misidentified conventional aircraft, celestial bodies and so forth. Some "abductions" probably have prosaic explanation, ranging from distorted recollections of rape or other trauma to outright delusion. Likewise, there are demonstrable cases of fraud, some very cleverly contrived. But the people in this first group, many of whom are scientists, hold that there is no evidence whatsoever to support claims of an alien presence on earth, past or present. In this book, Stanton Friedman addresses these people in no uncertain terms, arguing that their viewpoint — which seems to proceed from the assumption that an alien presence is impossible *a priori* — can only be based upon ignorance or willful denial of the facts. While many in this first group seem to be expressing sincere views, evidence indicates that some are simply lying. Indeed, denial and deception have characterized the official UFO cover-up since its inception in 1947.

Second, some UFO researchers believe that only a very small number of cases represent evidence of an alien presence. While agreeing, for example, that the Roswell incident is legitimate, they are inclined to see it as a rare and isolated event, evidence that intelligent beings do exist beyond the confines of earth, but not that such beings are here in significant numbers. I like to think of these people as the conservative wing of ufology. They are important in that they provide a much-needed corrective for others in the field whose enthusiasm runs at times toward credulity. Among the present interview subjects, Bob Lazar probably comes closest to this conservative view. On the other hand, his claims are hotly disputed by many in the conservative camp. All in all, the conservative viewpoint is not represented here.

Third, there are some people whose professed knowledge and experience of the alien presence is derived from channelled entities, telepathic communication and the like. These people often speak of a benign "space brotherhood" that watches over the plight of humanity and stands ready to assist in our eventual salvation. Some of them claim to have taken rides on alien craft in full waking consciousness, and to have dealt with alien beings that appear like "perfected humans." Famous contactees of the 1950s, such as George Adamski and George Van Tassel, and the more recent case of Billy Meier, epitomize this category. While it would be pleasant to discover that the adherents of space brotherhood are even partly correct, the best current evidence leads mainly in other directions. Thus, these people are not represented here, although the interview with Donald Ware does address some aspects of their viewpoint.

Finally, there are numerous researchers who belong to what I will call the liberal wing of ufology. I include myself in this group, along with those who speak in these pages. Within this group, the alien presence is generally regarded as having several important characteristics, among which are the following:

• The alien presence is real. Evidence overwhelmingly supports the basic claim that intelligent non-human beings are present on the earth.

• The alien presence is substantial. There are not just a few compelling cases, but hundreds or thousands, suggesting that alien entities are here in large numbers.

• The alien presence is active and purposeful. Evidence suggests that alien entities are engaged in a wide variety of activities, some involving human-alien contact, some involving other earth-based life-forms, geophysical experiments, and so forth. Many of their actions remain inscrutable, yet some kind of purpose must motivate them.

• The alien presence is diverse. Evidence suggests that more than one type of alien intelligence is functioning on earth. There may be dozens of different types, some related to and cooperative with one another, some perhaps wholly unrelated and even at odds with one another. Some of these beings are probably true extraterrestrials, visiting from a planet that circles a distant star. Some may actually be indigenous to the earth, yet belong to an order of being unrelated to humanity. Some may even traverse parallel dimensions to appear among us, only to disappear again (as often reported) through esoteric portals they alone can see.

• The alien presence is known to elite and secretive groups within the U.S. government, as well as other major governments. For a variety of reasons, those who know of it decided decades ago that public revelation of the alien presence posed an unacceptable risk to social order. Thus, the truth has been hidden behind the most aggressive and ingenious cover-up in history. It is possible that the nature of this cover-up has started to change in recent years. In any case, alien-related occurrences have become so numerous and visible that the cover-up is slowly being undone. How governments will respond to this development, over which they have very limited control, remains difficult to predict.

Although I believe all the voices in this book speak essentially from this "liberal" viewpoint on the alien presence, I do not mean to suggest that they are all in complete agreement. On the contrary, there are probably as many independent viewpoints on this complex subject as there are researchers and first-hand witnesses. Nor do I necessarily agree with everything said in the following pages. I do feel confident, however, that those who speak here have gone further than most other people toward understanding what is actually true in the matter of an alien presence on our planet, and that their willingness to speak out is a service to humanity.

There can be no doubt that human history is entering a new era. Assuming that much of the information in this book proves true — as I expect it will — the new era might well be characterized above all by the discovery of our place in the galactic community of intelligence. Such a discovery could bring many anxieties and discomforts in the short term. But perhaps, in the end, it will be exceedingly good news. Regardless, it is important for citizens the world over to recognize that we are not alone in the wide universe. Ignorance and willful denial of this stupendous fact must soon end. This book is offered as a contribution toward that goal.

Michael Lindemann
President, 2020 Group
May 25, 1991

Stanton Friedman

Chapter One
Stanton Friedman:
The Case for UFOs as Alien Spacecraft
and the Government UFO Cover-up

Stanton Friedman was born in New Jersey in 1934. He holds BS
and MS degrees in physics from the University of Chicago. As
a nuclear physicist, his past employers include General Electric, General Motors, Westinghouse, Aerojet General and TRW.

Stan is also one of the most distinguished and outspoken
UFO researchers in America, and probably the leading authority on the U.S. government's UFO cover-up. Among his many
contributions to UFO research, he discovered and investigated
the first leads that eventually revealed the Roswell, New Mexico
UFO crash-recovery of 1947, an event that had been successfully hidden from public awareness for thirty years. He has
published more than 50 papers about UFOs, appeared on
hundreds of radio and TV shows and lectured at over 600
colleges throughout the United States and Canada.

Ralph Steiner conducted the following interview with
Stan in San Francisco in May, 1990. Ralph and I later met
privately with Stan, again in the Bay Area, to discuss developments in a number of significant UFO cases. Despite his busy
schedule, Stan has been exceedingly generous with his time
and knowledge.

Readers wishing additional information from Stanton
Friedman can receive a free list of his published papers by
sending a self-addressed, stamped envelope to him at P.O. Box
958, Houlton, ME 04730. He can also be reached by phone at
506-457-0232. — ML

Ralph Steiner: How do we know UFOs are real? Why isn't there irrefutable evidence that science can agree with?

Stanton Friedman: The question isn't whether UFOs are real, the question is whether *any* UFOs are alien spacecraft. Even the biggest skeptics will say, "Of course there are UFOs, things that people see that they can't identify. But all of them have prosaic explanations."

Phil Klass, the aviation writer,[1] maintains that there are no sightings that he hasn't been able to explain. In the four anti-UFO books that he's written, he never even mentions the largest official government-sponsored scientific study ever done for the United States Air Force, *Project Bluebook Special Report 14*, which has data on 3,201 sightings, of which 21.5 percent, over 600 cases, could not be explained by professional people working for the Air Force. But Klass maintains, since he doesn't mention that in any of his books, that there are no cases without prosaic explanation.

The problem is that there's been very little effort on the part of the media and the scientific community to come to grips with the truth. We certainly are dealing with a "Cosmic Watergate." That is, the government has withheld the best data, and put cover stories all over the place to make getting at the truth all the more difficult. When you throw into that picture the "laughter curtain" that's been erected — one wonders whether it's intentional or not, but I suspect that it probably is — it takes a lot of courage to dig into the subject. There have only been eight Ph.D. theses done about UFOs, yet there's room for 80. So there aren't too many courageous professors around. I know of nobody who's a full-time UFO reporter for the major news media. They've got astrology columns, gardening columns, all kinds of other things, but no UFO reporter. And yet, there are loads of sightings going on all the time.

The case for flying saucer reality is far better than the case against most convicted criminals. If you do it on an evidential basis, you can look at things like Ted Phillips' collected information on over 4,400 physical trace cases from 66 countries.[2]

These are cases where the saucer is seen on or near the ground, and after it leaves, one finds clear physical changes such as burn circles and burn rings, landing gear marks, swirled vegetation, dried out soil, and so forth. People say there is no physical evidence. Well, if a footprint and a fingerprint are physical evidence, then the physical trace cases are certainly physical evidence. And the same things keep happening all over the world.

The problem is, most people are unaware of the evidence. The people who could do you the most good are the most unaware, comparatively speaking. I've lectured at over 600 colleges in 50 states, 8 Canadian provinces, and a few foreign countries. I check my audiences, and typically, fewer than two percent of the people have read any of the five major scientific studies on UFOs that I talk about. That's an indication that we're dealing with people who are very ignorant on this subject.

Then throw in the laughter problem, and as far as they're concerned, there's nothing to dig into. They certainly don't want to get their feet wet in something that could only lead to ridicule. This is despite the fact that polls have consistently shown that most people do believe in UFOs, and the greater their education, the more likely their belief. But everybody acts as if they don't believe in UFOs, because they think most other people don't. In my audiences, typically 10% of the people have seen a UFO. But when I ask how many have reported what they've seen, I get maybe one in 20, of that 10%. Their concern almost invariably is, "I said something to somebody and they laughed and gave me a hard time, so why should I say anything to anybody else?"

RS: Why is the phenomenon so elusive?

SF: I don't see what's elusive about the phenomenon. You take any large group of people, and you'll find sightings in that group of people. That's exactly the opposite of elusive. I found it interesting that skeptic-debunker Phil Klass tried in his first book to explain UFOs as ball lightning. But far more people have seen UFOs than have seen real ball lightning.

RS: What level of proof is adequate proof, then?

SF: I talk in terms of evidence. The legal profession recognizes certain standards: in a civil court, "preponderance of the evidence;" in a criminal court, "beyond a reasonable doubt." I think there is, right now, quite sufficient evidence. Given the physical trace cases, the radar sightings, the photographs and the eye-witness testimony from people all over the world, we have quite sufficient evidence to conclude that our planet is being visited by manufactured objects behaving in ways that we Earthlings cannot yet duplicate, and that therefore were produced someplace else. Now, the reason for that little kicker about not being able to duplicate: every government in the world would love to be able to duplicate UFO flying capabilities. If we could build these things, we would be building them. But we're not. We're still building F-16s and F-18s, and Russian MiG-29s and French Mirages.[3] So, if they weren't built here, they were built someplace else. There's nothing exotic about that. It's not charismatic handwaving, it's perfectly good reasoning. We have an adequate amount of evidence today to clearly establish that some — I emphasize *some* — UFOs are alien spacecraft. And I would take on anybody who says we don't. I would say it's entirely because they haven't reviewed that evidence, which is very different from saying there is no evidence.

RS: Give me some examples. What are some of the strongest cases on record that you know of, and why do you find them so convincing?

SF: I feel the Roswell evidence makes a very strong case. We've talked to more than 240 people about that case; people at the Roswell Army Air Force base; people out at the rancher's site, including Mac Brazel's neighbors, his son, his daughter, and his daughter-in-law. We've talked to people who handled pieces of the wreckage at the base; we've talked to the people who were in Texas where it went; people who were crew members on the planes that carried some of the wreckage. I've talked to somebody who saw the bodies, people who were threatened by the government — that's being kind — to shut up about this whole thing. So that's an excellent case.

But I'm also impressed by cases like the one that occurred over George Air Force Base in California.[4] Two jets had just finished maneuvering practice and were coming back to base. Both were flown by experienced pilots who had fought in Korea. The pilot in the lead plane spotted an object in the distance. It looked peculiar because it was standing still, so he radioed the ground. The ground control guy went outside with binoculars and watched the two planes go after this thing, meanwhile still talking to them by radio. And, as the lead pilot reported, the object was standing still, and in three seconds it was going a thousand miles an hour. It moved a pretty good angle through the sky, then stopped dead again. The pilot switched direction a little bit, going after it, and it went back the other way. Again, in just a couple seconds of acceleration, it's going, he says, a thousand miles an hour. Stops dead. Zigzagging, in other words, back and forth across the sky. The lead pilot saw it, the pilot in the second plane saw it, and the guy on the ground watched this whole thing while listening to the radio conversations. Finally, the thing zipped away at very high speed. Now, what do you do with a case like that? These are military pilots reporting to a military control tower operator in broad daylight. You can't say they're lying. What for? This was a classified report. It makes no sense. And there are loads of cases like that.

I'm also impressed with some of the abduction cases; for example, the Betty and Barney Hill case [see Briefing, next page]. I was technical advisor on a television movie about this case called "The UFO Incident," and I've spent time with the Hills. These two people underwent individual medical hypnosis sessions weekly for three and a half months. Betty was a social worker and supervisor in the welfare department, State of New Hampshire. Barney worked for the Post Office and was on the Governor's Civil Rights Commission. Our whole society would fall apart if we had to say that people like this who report anything strange must either be nuts or else have some crazy angle to what they're doing. We have standard procedures for accepting eye-witness testimony. These people and lots of other abductees certainly meet those standards for providing acceptable testimony.

So, I get irked when I hear people say there isn't any evidence. We've got things like the University of Colorado study, the Condon Report, in which 30% of 117 cases studied in detail couldn't be identified.[5] *Bluebook Special Report 14* does a cross-comparison between 600-plus *unknowns* and the balance of 2000-plus cases that could be identified. They looked at six different characteristics — apparent size, color, shape, speed, etc. — to see if there was any chance that the unknowns were just missed knowns. It was less than one percent. They did a

BRIEFING:

The Abduction of Betty and Barney Hill

The first widely reported case of alleged alien abduction took place at about 2:00 am on September 20, 1961. Betty and Barney Hill were driving south on Route 3 near the town of Lincoln, New Hampshire, when they noticed a strange object in the sky. After watching the object from their car for several minutes, they stopped, got out and observed it with binoculars. They later reported that the object approached to within a few hundred feet, by which time it appeared to be a flying machine of unknown origin.

The Hills could see windows in the craft, and behind the windows, humanoid beings looking at them. During this time, both the Hills experienced short bursts of loud buzzing in their heads. They became frightened and quickly drove away, arriving soon after at the town of Ashland, about 35 miles to the south. Only later did they realize that they could not account for two hours of time, nor could they consciously remember driving the distance to Ashland.

After the sighting, Betty and Barney both experienced disturbing nightmares and decided to see a psychiatrist. In separate sessions, each of them underwent hypnotic regression to recall details of the experience. Their stories matched in most respects. They said that beings from the craft had approached their car and taken them aboard. They were led to separate rooms, where each underwent examination. Betty reported that a long needle was inserted into her abdomen. She asked its purpose and was told it was a pregnancy test. At the time of her report, the medical procedure called amniocentesis had not yet been invented.

Betty described her examiners as about five feet tall, with bluish-gray skin, dark hair and large noses, "like Jimmy Durante." She thought their features looked somewhat mongoloid, and their eyes looked like those of a cat. Barney described his examiners as having large craniums that narrowed to small chins, metallic gray skin and large eyes that "continued around to the sides of their heads." They had no visible hair and almost no nose, only slits for nostrils. These differences in Betty and Barney's reports proved significant in later years, as mounting numbers of witnesses implicated both the "big-nosed" and the "big-eyed" types of gray entities in alleged abduction episodes.

In *Dimensions: A Casebook of Alien Contact* (Ballantine pbk edition, 1989, p.103ff) veteran UFO researcher Jacques Vallee reveals the little-known fact that military radar at Pease Air Force Base in New Hampshire had recorded the object seen by the Hills that night. The most complete description of the Hill abduction and its aftermath can be found in *The Interrupted Journey* by John Fuller (Dial Press, 1966). — ML

quality evaluation. They found that the better the quality, the more likely to be an unknown. That's exactly what you'd expect if we're dealing with something different. Because they had other categories: not only "unknown," but insufficient information, aircraft, astronomical, balloon, psychological aberrations. The unknowns were different. And the differences were in the direction of being able to move with much greater maneuverability and much greater speed, to have a different shape, to have different lighting. What do people want? We're dealing with vehicles in the air, many of them observed in the early 1950s or late '40s, doing things that we certainly could not do. So, the evidence, for anybody who wants to take the time, — and it does take time — is overwhelming that *some* UFOs are alien spacecraft and that we're dealing with a kind of "Cosmic Watergate." No question.

RS: Some people have suggested that perhaps some sort of psychological or deep mythological answer can be given to all this, that these are projections of the collective unconscious, as Carl Jung described in 1958, or even that these are emanations, somehow, of a psychic nature. What's your response to that?

SF: The simplest response is balderdash. I'm not saying that there's not a psychic aspect to all this. I would be astonished if advanced alien civilizations, who are able to casually get here and who could be a billion years ahead of us — because we know there are stars out there that are five billion years older than the sun, much less a billion — didn't understand the world of the mind. We're just getting there. There are several things you could assume they would know about with advanced technology. One is biology. That seems natural, because you have to control disease, you have to find out about feeding people. You'd learn about aging as a natural part of that, and if you learn about aging, you're going to live longer because you control it. And if you're going to live longer, and have access to good computers, you're going to be able to learn a great deal, so you'd expect wisdom. So the notion that an advanced civilization, men, women or whatever, isn't going to dig into these other areas, doesn't make any sense to me.

I think all of these theorists are stuck with a problem. Because they haven't worked on advanced technology, because they don't know how relatively easy it is to travel between the stars, they've got to come up with another explanation. They know that not everybody's making up stories. People are obviously seeing something that doesn't fit. What could it be? Well, assuming you can't get here from there, it must be from another dimension, a parallel universe. Or it's a psychic projection, a mythological what-have-you. They'll bring up the faeries that were seen in Ireland. But the case for the flying saucer rests on good, solid evidence. Why are they fighting that some UFOs are alien spacecraft?

The question I'm asking is not, "Are *all* UFOs alien spacecraft?" That's a stupid question. It's as confusing as it must have been to the American Indian. "Are all the white men from England?" Well, no, 300 years ago there were some from Spain, some from Portugal, some from Holland and half a dozen other countries. "Are all the white men here to kill us?" No, there were some to convert them, some to steal from them. There were all kinds of motivations. So, to try to put into one box, what are flying saucers, or what are UFOs, is silly. It seems to me that you have to ask the right question. We have every manifestation that we're dealing with manufactured vehicles with beings on board — 24% of the 4,400 physical trace cases that Ted Phillips has collected have involved reports of creatures associated with the craft, including dozens of cases of small footprints. What are we supposed to do with this? The notion that this is a conspiracy, as one guy suggested — "the CIA is hiring midgets to run around playing humanoids" — is absurd on its face.

RS: Give me examples of how prevalent the sightings of humanoids are.

SF: The humanoid study group of the Mutual UFO Network has collected well over 3,000 reports of humanoids. We've got well over a thousand abduction cases that have been checked into, almost all of which involve reports of humanoids. By that I mean two arms, two legs, a head and a body, but not like us. There are other cases with beings more or less like us. Now, if people are reluctant to report a dumb old UFO sighting, and maybe only one in 20 does, then how much more reluctant are they to report seeing a strange character with the UFO? "Something landed in our back yard and this little guy got out." You've got to be real gutsy to report that. There are plenty of such cases, but what I'm saying is, we've only got the tip of the iceberg here.

RS: We also have a situation of extremely high strangeness associated with a lot of UFO sightings. Stories where people are floated through walls by aliens, or where beings seem to just appear in a room and then disappear — things that are absolutely fantastic. And yet, some of these abduction cases are among the most reputable ones. How do you account for that?

SF: Arthur C. Clarke once said it very well: "Advanced technology is by definition magic." If you tried to show your great-great grandfather a television set, it would have been magic. Utterly impossible. There must be midgets inside. And yet, when humans landed on the moon — a remarkable thing in itself — we could watch it in real time, as it happened. Quite extraordinary. A pocket calculator today represents an enormously sophisticated kind of device. What about a hologram? You want crazy stuff! If you've ever seen a big hologram, you know you can put your hand through the darn thing, but it sure looks like there's something there. That's magic.

So, what I'm saying is, I don't have the faintest idea how to float somebody through a wall, but the way of science is to recognize that the observations are real, though the explanations may be all wet. And that's a problem for a number of ancient academics, fossilized physicists. If they don't understand how something happens, it can't be. The sun has been fusioning up there, the primary source of energy for all our society, since the beginning. We figured out in 1937-38 how the sun works, that it's fusion, not burning gas. But could anybody in his right mind suggest that it was fusioning until we knew about fusion? Of course not. So, you have to have a tolerance for ambiguity, for mystery, and a recognition that there are things we don't know. The more questions we ask, the more we don't know, because there's more we can dig into. The true scientist recognizes that. He'll say, "Gee, that's intriguing, that's different, how could we do that?" The false scientist says, "That's impossible, I'm going to ignore it." I'm reminded of Simon Newcomb, a great American astronomer of the 19th century, who published in October, 1903, a long detailed paper considering the possibility of man flying in a vehicle. His conclusion was that the only way man would ever fly would be in a lighter-than-air vehicle, a balloon. This was two months before the Wright Brothers' first flight, and when told about that, he said, "Well, maybe a pilot, but it'll never carry a passenger." He didn't know anything about flight. It's the basic assumptions that mattered. A little over 20 years later, another great astronomer "proved" it would be impossible to give anything sufficient energy to get it into orbit around the earth. All he proved was that he had made the wrong assumptions. Finally, the example that kind of teases me the most is Dr. Campbell, a great Canadian astronomer, who published in 1941 a long detailed paper proving that the required initial launch weight of a chemical rocket able to get a man to the moon and back would be a million-million tons. We accomplished it less than thirty years later, with a dumb old chemical rocket whose initial launch weight was 3,000 tons. He was off by a factor of 300 million. Why? Because he didn't know anything about space flight! All his assumptions were wrong.

We're stupid, we're silly, we're ridiculous, we're unprofessional. And that's the kicker here. Because we don't have explanations, because we cannot duplicate, doesn't mean that it cannot happen. Friedman's Law, if you will: technological advancement almost invariably comes from doing things differently in an unpredictable way. The future is not an extrapolation of the past. A great scientist, Max Planck, once said, "New ideas come to be accepted, not because their opponents come to believe in them, but because their opponents die and a new generation grows up that's accustomed to them." So, I get upset at professional people who put their pride before their science. They can't figure out how something could happen, so it couldn't, and that's the end of that. And that's not science, that's pseudo-science.

RS: Let's talk about the official U.S. policy concerning this subject.

SF: It's kind of funny. Lots of people ask, "How come the Air Force says there are no flying saucers? How come the government says there are no flying saucers?" The Air Force doesn't say that, and the government doesn't say that. In December, 1969, when the Air Force closed Project Bluebook, which we now know was one of many government groups concerned with UFOs, they made three statements, none of which was, "There are no flying saucers." Their first statement was, "No UFO sighting reported, evaluated or investigated by the United States Air Force gives any evidence of being a threat to the security of the United States." That sounds very impressive, but what does it mean? The penguins in Antarctica aren't a threat to the security of the United States, but they're certainly real. What if any of those three functions were done by somebody else, such as the NSA, the CIA, the DIA, the NRO, or any of the other alphabet-soup intelligence agencies? If they were doing any one of these things, the statement could be true but totally meaningless.

The second thing they said: "The United States Air Force does not have in its possession the equivalent of physical artifacts." Well, what does that mean? Why should they have it? If any of those other agencies have it, it could be a true statement, but it doesn't mean there aren't any. Also, incidentally, having been involved in classified projects for almost fifteen years, if the existence of those things was classified, they'd have to lie about them anyway. You have to lie when people are touching on classified matters.

The third thing they said: "There is no evidence of technology beyond our knowledge." What the heck does that mean? I worked on fusion propulsion systems for deep space travel almost thirty years ago. If you use the right stuff in the right way, you can kick particles out the back end of a fusion rocket with 10 million times as much energy per particle as you can get in a dumb old chemical rocket. The fact that we haven't done it yet doesn't mean we don't know about it. So, when you look at those three statements, they do not at all mean that there are no flying saucers, or that there have been no crashed saucers. They mean what they say, which is darn little.

We certainly know, from following up on Freedom of Information requests for example, that all the intelligence agencies were heavily involved in collecting data about flying saucers. We know that the National Security Agency, the CIA,

the Air Force and Naval Intelligence are all withholding documents. There is clearly a major policy of the United States
government to only release a very limited amount of information about flying saucers. J. Edgar Hoover himself, while head
of the FBI, wrote letters to people who sent in requests for
information about UFOs: "It is not now, nor has it ever been, the
role of the FBI to investigate UFO sightings." But then we got
more than 2,000 pages of information from the FBI, indicating
that they were up to their ears in UFO information.

We got the distribution list for a memo from the military
attache in Teheran, before the Shah's overthrow, back to Washington. The memo reports an excellent case over there. Two
American F-4 jets with Iranian pilots went after a UFO and had
their systems conk out — it was quite spectacular — and the
head of the Iranian Air Defense Command had seen the thing
himself before he ordered these guys up. And they were all
debriefed. Just looking at the distribution list, it's a dead
giveaway that this is a topic of major concern. The Com-
mander-in-Chief of the Pacific Fleet, and the Atlantic Fleet, and
everybody and his brother was getting this stuff. And everybody and his brother has lied.

Those Americans who can't believe that secrets can be
kept might consider that the annual "black budget" — that's
the budget not under Congressional control, pulled from hither,
thither and yon — according to a Pulitzer Prize-winning series
of articles in the *Philadelphia Inquirer*[6], is 35 billion dollars. The
annual black budget of the National Security Agency is supposedly running at ten billion dollars. And yet, more than half
the people in my college audiences have never heard of the
NSA. So, anybody who thinks you can't keep secrets doesn't
know what he or she is talking about. Secrets can be kept and
are being kept. And that's not all bad, incidentally.

RS: Why are they keeping it a secret?

SF: That's a different question, of course. I'll give you several
reasons why all governments are keeping it secret. You see, it's

not just the United States government, it's a worldwide phenomenon. Some people might think I'm saying there's a conspiracy. I'm not saying that at all, although there may be. But I am saying that there are sometimes common interests. People may be enemies and still think the same way about things. Here are several good reasons for all governments to not want to put the UFO data out on the table:

First, they want to figure out how the darn things work. As a top-secret Canadian document said in 1950, "Modus operandi is as yet unknown."[7] You've got pieces, you've got wreckage. You set up your secret project, say, a small group working under Dr. Vannevar Bush, the top science administrator during and after World War II in the United States. The first problem is, you want to figure out how they work. Rule number one is security. You can't tell your friends without telling your enemies. I mean, they read the newspapers too, listen to the radio, watch television.

Second, the other side of the same coin: What happens if somebody else figures out how they work before you do? They'd make wonderful weapons delivery and defense systems. You don't want them to know you know they know. Because, you see, if the technology is unusual, there may be ways of countering that, as long as they don't know you know. It's like poison gas. If you've got poison gas and I've got the antidote and you find out I've got the antidote, you're going to change your poison gas. Then I've got to change my antidote, and so forth. This whole sequence has been going on for thousands of years. Stronger shields, bigger spears, swords and all the rest.

Third, and very important: the political problem. Suppose there were to be an announcement tomorrow by highly trusted individuals around the world, George Bush and Mr. Gorbachev maybe, or the Pope and the Queen — you know, pick your own odd couple — saying that, indeed, some UFOs are alien spacecraft. What would happen? Well, you know darn well the stock market would go down, church attendance and mental hospital admissions would go up. But the big thing that would happen, I believe, is that there would be an immediate push on the part of the younger generation, never alive when there wasn't a space program, for a whole new view of ourselves. Instead of Americans, Russians, Chinese, Paraguayans — just Earthlings. Because obviously, from an alien viewpoint, we are all Earthlings, even though we tend to forget it most of the time.

Gee, you say, that would be great. We could solve all the world's problems — the environmental problems, the political problems — if we all thought of ourselves as Earthlings. But then you realize that there isn't any government on this planet that wants its citizens to owe their primary allegiance to the planet. Nationalism is the only game in town. That's why we spent a trillion dollars last year on things military, in the name of nationalism, protecting ourselves against the other guy, or preparing to attack the other guy, depending on where you sit.

And there's a fourth problem, the religious one. There are a number of fundamentalists who believe that this is the work of the devil, that man is the only intelligent life in the universe. And the rug would be pulled out from under them. And you may recall that on occasion the government has been influenced strongly by fundamentalists. Reagan certainly was.

Then there's the fifth problem: economic discumbobulation, if you will. If the public perception, when an announcement was made, was that there would be new means of transportation, new means of energy production, new medical things — a whole new world — there would be a tremendous loss in the stock value of oil companies, power companies, car companies, plane companies. I mean, forget psychological panic; that's a different story. There's still five percent of the people in the United States who don't believe we've been to the Moon. But the economic problems that might arise, should an announcement be made — that's a big difficulty. How do you handle that? It's kind of like we're seeing right now with regard to Eastern Europe. "Freedom, freedom, they won their freedom." But that doesn't convert you from a really second-rate economy into a capitalist economy. Now you've got freedom, but how do you get from A to B? As we're finding out, it's not easy.

And so, even though people might easily accept, as I think they would, the notion of alien spacecraft — most people already do, according to the polls — that doesn't mean the transition is without its difficulties. Certainly, the government would have asked psychiatrists and social scientists what would happen, and they'd say, "Well, it depends on how you broach the announcement. You could make it 'Fear, fear, fear!' Or you could make it 'just' difficulty for religion, economics, politics, medicine, industry. You have a choice." And I think for many governments, the natural thing to do is to postpone the decision. Let somebody else worry about it. It's a big problem, and I can understand the reluctance.

However, I must add that, as a nuclear physicist very much concerned about the proliferation of nuclear weapons amongst countries that I wouldn't trust with a bazooka, much less a nuclear weapon, the only hope I see for a decent future for this planet is an Earthling orientation. By far the easiest way to get that is to recognize that there *are* aliens coming here.

RS: How is it possible that this government could have completely covered up a story as earth-shaking as this for four decades?

SF: I think it's extraordinarily easy. In the first place, the good tools for getting the best data all belong to the government. They've got the radar systems, the closed communication systems, the aircraft loaded with instrumentation, the Air Defense Command and so forth. And all that data is born classified. If you were to ask me as a physicist what I'd like to do to find out about flying saucers, I'd say, well, you've got to have a system to detect them, then you need another system to monitor them once you've picked one up, then you want to communicate back and forth and get guys up there with instruments as close as you can when they're there. The government's got all of that, and it's all classified. So, that's the first thing: they've got a closed system to begin with.

Secondly, when we talk government, we imply — at least some people do — that everybody knows and nobody's talking. That's not how security works at all. I had a clearance for fifteen years. The "need to know" concept is most important. As an example of that, I was working on radiation shielding for nuclear airplanes for General Electric. I would have liked access to secret restricted data on radiation shielding being produced by Westinghouse for the nuclear submarine program. I mean, a shield is a shield. You've got the same difficulties with light weight and that sort of thing. I didn't have a need-to-know for their data. I had the right level of clearance, but it got me nowhere. So, the key is compartmentalization, which was honed to a science during World War II by some of the same people who were apparently involved with UFOs post-war. How did we keep the Manhattan Project secret as long as we did? Two billion dollars in 1942 money, tens of thousands of people involved in the construction of enormous facilities that at one point were using eleven percent of the electricity in the United States, to blow uranium hexaflouride through little holes in a mile-long building — and yet, it was kept secret. Secrets are easy to keep, as long as you control the detection systems, the communications systems, and the interference systems, if you will. I've talked to a number of people who worked for Truman and Eisenhower. Every single one agreed that secrets could have always been kept, at least post-World War II. No problem at all.

RS: So now we suspect there's a cover-up. What evidence do we have that that's the case?

SF: It's easy to make the case for the U.S. government cover-up. A group called Citizens Against UFO Secrecy went after the CIA for their UFO information. We went through all the legal steps, because the CIA said they had nothing, nothing, nothing. We appeal, they deny, we go to court. They throw us 800 pages — but nothing above secret, which in itself is suspicious, because I've looked at enough intelligence files to know there were loads of top-secret material in them. This stuff was mildly interesting. It contained internal references to other documents that weren't there. More importantly, they give us a list of 57 documents originating with other agencies. Everybody and his brother was collecting UFO data.

Eighteen documents were from the super-secret National Security Agency. Naturally, we filed a Freedom of Information request for them. This was a decade ago. They came back to us saying, "Go away, don't bother us, we don't give anything to anybody." We appeal, they deny, we go to court. The judge asked the NSA to do a document search, with us knowing about only 18 documents. They came back to court. "How many UFO documents did you find, gentlemen?" "Uh, 239, your honor." But 79 originated with this whole long list of other agencies, 23 from the CIA, which is where we started on this quest. That leaves 160. They condensed it to 156. "Fine," we said, "we'll take 156 NSA UFO documents." "You can't have anything. We cannot give you any of these documents."

We were going around in circles, so we tried a legal ploy. We asked that they show those documents to the judge. The point was that in other cases, judges have been asked to rule on whether the agency claiming national security as a reason for not releasing information was properly invoking national security, as opposed to protecting themselves against embarrassment. They refused to show anything to the judge, but they did provide him with a 21-page top-secret affidavit justifying the withholding of these 156 NSA UFO documents. He was so impressed — he saw this in chambers; our lawyer didn't get to see it — that he ruled in their favor. They shouldn't release the data. And he said that the public interest in disclosure is far outweighed by the potential danger to the security of the United States, were this information to be released. National security and flying saucers. We appealed to the Federal Court of Appeals, which normally takes two months to reach a decision. Five days after being shown this same 21-page top-secret affidavit, they agreed with the lower court. We tried to go to the Supreme Court. They wouldn't hear the case. Naturally, we filed a Freedom of Information request for the 21-page top-secret affidavit from the NSA, and eventually we got it. As we started to go through it, it was laughable, because 75% of that document isn't there. It's blacked out entirely.

Anybody who says the government isn't keeping secrets from the public about UFOs is absolutely wrong, judging by the government documents themselves and the ruling of a Federal Court judge. Now, there's a footnote to this story that's kind of funny. Naturally, I filed a Freedom of Information request to the CIA for their 23 UFO documents, as picked up by the NSA and somehow missed by the CIA. Thirty-five months later I got a response. They agreed to release the first nine, which — believe it or not — were press abstracts of Eastern European newspaper articles about UFOs, which presumably the Russians had seen the day they were published. They withheld their own 14. I appealed that decision. Two years later, I got a response. They withheld eleven in their entirety. They released portions of three. I say portions, but I mean extraordinarily small portions. You get a page that's almost all blacked out except for six words. In one of them, it was ten words. Things like date, USSR, September — these words were there. Everything else, including the security markings, were blacked out. And this is as a result of my appeal, so I can't go any farther. Now, I've been challenging the UFO debunkers for years: get me *any* of those 156 NSA documents, get me *any* of these newly-noted CIA UFO documents. I'm still waiting.

I should add that there's a little history here that most people aren't aware of. Most people have probably heard that the CIA was involved in some rather nasty mind-control experiments — using LSD, people commiting suicide, conditioning of all kinds of people up in Canada and in the United States. As a matter of fact, a legal suit was just settled on that. This took place a long time ago.[8] I talked to the lawyer who was responsible for digging that stuff out, John Marks, and I asked him about how he got the stuff from them. Well, on his first request, they gave him 400 pages of material. He yelled and screamed, and he was a lawyer in Washington, so he could threaten to go to court. Just before he was going to go to court, they found another box. And then another box. And then another box. To make a long story short, he wound up with 40,000 pages of material. And the best stuff was in the last few thousand pages, amazingly enough. So, anybody who thinks that these guys play fair and square on Freedom of Information is wrong.

Incidentally, I've spent time at fourteen archives, and loads of stuff from the late 1940s and early '50s is still classified today. A good example is the Psychological Strategy Board, a CIA outfit that closed up shop in 1953. Their files were just re-reviewed within the past six months. Half that stuff is still classified. I was looking at Air Force headquarters files, and again, a majority of the stuff from the late '40s and early '50s is still classified. It's easy to keep secrets.

RS: When the government decides to release some stuff to you, how do you know what's true? It's often charged that informants who have come forward with UFO information are spreading disinformation. How does a researcher deal with the possibility that what you're getting is a lot of baloney?

SF: It's always a possibility. It depends on where you get it from. For example, at the Eisenhower library, there are 250,000 pages of National Security Council material. None of the people there have read all that stuff. It's in loads and loads of archive boxes. So, if you go to that archive, look at the finder's aids, and request certain boxes — and they don't know what you're going to ask for when you get there — you can be reasonably sure that you're getting what's there. It's funny. You find references to other documents, and they can't even find the other documents. So, when you get documents that way, you can be reasonably sure.

The Operation Majestic 12 documents, on the other hand, two out of three of which came in the form of a roll of film in the mail — there you've got a problem. You have to validate them. You have to see whether the information on those documents is legitimate, whether anybody on the outside could have faked it, whether you can find something that throws them out.

You always try to prove documents are frauds, which is very different from trying to prove they're true. How do you prove they're true? Even if it's the right paper, the right typewriter, that doesn't prove the information is right, because we know that over the years the CIA and other government agencies have put out lots of disinformation. The CIA has admitted that some of the stories it sent overseas came back as if they were fact. This has happened in recent years, for example, with regard to Kadafi and what he was preparing to do. A story came back to bite them. So, you do have to be careful.

My whole approach to this thing is "trust, but verify." That's why I've spent so much time at archives, and frankly why I have so little tolerance for the nasty, noisy negativism of those armchair theorists who don't go to the archives. They'll tell you, "That security marking isn't right. Those guys didn't use it." Well, if they'd ever been to an archive, they'd find that there might have been eight different security markings, some of which you don't see very often. That doesn't mean they're illigitimate. Format, style, everything in government documents varies all over the place. So, verification is not easy, and you have to maintain what I call a "gray basket." Until you get more information, "I don't know" is the proper response. Of course, you have to throw out the junk that you prove is phoney, and I've found some. But this is not the kind of thing that can be done quickly, by phone or by mail. You've got to go in there and look at the stuff.

RS: Would you say, then, that the arena for UFO research now is to try to pry open what our own government isn't telling us?

SF: Yes. People wonder what we should do about getting more information about UFOs. Investigating another light in the sky doesn't excite me at all. The government has got far more capability than any of our civilian groups do. So, the question now is to try to pry it out of them. The one good thing is that many of the people who are the custodians, so to speak, of the early stuff, weren't *involved* with the early stuff. So, they might make a mistake. This has happened on occasion. You get some words leaked out and you follow up on them. But it's a hard, time-consuming, frustrating, expensive job. The average time for the National Security Council to respond to a mandatory classification review request from the Eisenhower Library is running two and a half years, sometimes as long as six years. And you don't even know what you're asking for. All you have is a date and maybe a "Jones to Smith, Top Secret, three pages." You don't know what it is. So, it's slow, painstaking research.

RS: Let's move on to perhaps the biggest cover-up in human history. What happened July 2, 1947 in New Mexico, and how did you decide to start looking into it?

SF: It's been a long, slow process trying to unravel what happened in New Mexico in 1947. The government cover-up was quite effective.

Let me first explain how I got involved. I was writing articles with a woman friend of mine in California. She talked to a forest ranger who'd had a UFO sighting. When they finished, he said, "Gee, you really ought to talk to my mom. She had a much better sighting and she knows about this stuff." So we talked to the mom, Lydia Sleppy by name. She told us about her sighting, and it was run-of-the-mill, like lots of other sightings. But she also mentioned that she had been working for a radio station in Albuquerque in 1947. They'd gotten a call from their affiliate in Roswell, a guy down there telling her that a flying saucer had been recovered and was being sent to Wright Field. And he dictated a story to put out on the wire. She started to type it into the teletype, and the transmission was interrupted: "Do not continue this transmission." So she stopped. When she talked to the guy later, he was shut up and wouldn't tell her anything more. I heard this story in the mid-1970s. I tracked down a couple of people — she remembered some names — and I got stonewalled. Okay, it's one you file off to the side.

In 1978, I was down in Baton Rouge, Louisiana, to speak at Louisiana State University. I was at one of the local television stations, having coffee with the station manager, and he said, "The guy you really want to talk to is Jesse Marcel. He was a military guy, and he's a ham radio buddy of mine. He handled pieces of one of these things." *That* was an intriguing statement. So, the next day I called Jesse.

He told me that when he was the base intelligence officer at Roswell Army Air Force Base, Roswell, New Mexico — he didn't have a precise date — he got called by the local sheriff, to whose office a rancher had brought some strange material. The sheriff, by previous arrangement, called the base, which was the home of the 509th Composite Bomb Wing, the only atomic bombing group in the world. High level people, high level clearances — a very special, unique group of guys. Jesse told me that he and a counter-intelligence guy that everybody called Cav, Cavitt — we didn't even know what his first name was at that point — went out and talked to the rancher and stayed overnight. The next morning, the rancher showed them the wreckage that he had found. Here was an area three-quarters of a mile long, a quarter-mile wide, strewn with pieces of the craziest stuff he had ever seen. A lot of it was a kind of foil-like material about the thickness and weight of the foil on a package of cigarettes, but incredibly strong. They couldn't tear it, couldn't permanently crease it, couldn't break through it with a sledge hammer. This was weird stuff. In addition, there were some I-beam-like pieces about the weight of balsa wood that couldn't be cut, burned or broken, and that had strange symbols along the side. Anyway, the rancher showed them the stuff, and they took as much as they could, which was a very small fraction of what was there, in a Buick and an army carryall back to Roswell. Jesse Marcel stopped at home very late that night and woke up his eleven-year-old son and his wife. They tried to fit pieces of this stuff together, with no luck, on the kitchen table.

The son, who has also testified about this event, is Doctor

Jesse Marcel. Not only is he a medical doctor, but he's a pilot of fixed-wing and helicopter aircraft, and he served on a number of military aircraft accident investigation teams. Wreckage is no stranger to him. And he's never seen anything like those symbols or that material.

Jesse told me that the base commander gave him instructions the next morning to fly this stuff up to Wright Field — Air Materiel Command is where you send all captured enemy equipment, incidentally — and to stop at the headquarters of the Eighth Air Force in Fort Worth, Texas, on the way up. In other words, "Let the head of the Eighth Air Force (their bosses, so to speak) worry about it, not me." The base commander also gave a second order to Walter Haut, base public information officer, to put out a press release saying we've now captured — "recovered" would be a better word — one of these flying disks that people have been seeing all over the country the last couple of weeks.[9] Walter did that, and by the time Jesse got to Texas, newsmen all over the world were calling New Mexico. Not only were they calling the base, they were calling the local sheriff's office — I've talked to his daughter. They were calling the editor of the paper — I've talked to him. And I've talked to Walter Haut. There was a lot of attention around the world when this announcement came out.

By the time Jesse's plane got to Fort Worth, the fix was already in. I've talked to retired Air Force General Thomas Jefferson Dubose, then a colonel, who was the Chief of Staff to General Roger Ramey, head of the Eighth Air Force. Colonel Dubose took a call from a man named Clemence McMullen, a three-star general who basically was running the Strategic Air Command, of which they were a part, headquartered at that time at Andrews Air Force Base in Washington, DC. McMullen told Colonel Dubose in no uncertain terms to cover this up. "I don't want to hear anything about this, I don't want you even to talk to your friend Roger Ramey about this, Colonel. That's an order. Do I need to put it in writing?" "No, sir." "And another order: get one of your colonel couriers to fly some of that wreckage back here today." "Yes, sir." This man's still alive, as of a couple of months ago. I've been in his home.

We have now met with an effective coverup. General Ramey took the easy way out: "Gentlemen, we made a terrible mistake. It isn't one of these flying disks at all, it was just the radar reflector from a weather balloon." And he brought in the base weather officer, Irving Newton — I've talked to him — and ordered him to identify the wreckage of a weather balloon. It wasn't the real wreckage at all. The real wreckage was taken off the plane under guard, put on another plane and sent up to Wright Field, while the first plane was sent back to Roswell. We have an FBI memo that establishes that.

My colleagues and I now have talked to a total of 240 people or so about Roswell. Basically, what happened is that a saucer flew over Roswell, a rancher heard an enormous explosion at night, and the next day, July 3, he and his daughter found some of his fields strewn with wreckage. A few days later, they went into town. They were out in the boonies, 75 or 85 miles northwest of Roswell, with the nearest neighbor ten miles away. Once in town, they talked to the sheriff, and that's where this story unfolds.

RS: Let me clarify. Are you saying that you have an FBI memo attesting to the fact that this extraordinary material was moved to Wright-Patterson?

SF: Yes. And that it was not part of a weather balloon, although that's what the public was told.

RS: What does the memo say it is?

SF: It doesn't say what it is.

RS: How does it list it? How does it describe it?

SF: Well, it's from the Special Agent in Charge, Dallas, to the Special Agent in Charge, Cincinnati — which is next to Dayton, Dallas being next to Fort Worth — saying that there was a lot of media interest in this thing, and that what was thought to be a weather balloon turns out not to be a weather balloon. It's being sent to Wright Field for analysis. It doesn't say much more. It's less than one page, sort of telegram format. My colleagues have talked to the guy who wrote the memo; I found him. He's one of the very few people we approached who said, "Happy in my retirement. No guys in black suits on my doorstep. I cannot talk to you." Which was an interesting response indeed.

RS: So he appeared to know about the guys in black suits.

SF: Well, he certainly was aware that he shouldn't open his mouth. Apparently he'd been debriefed. As a matter of fact, eventually we found the Counterintelligence Corps guy who went out with Jesse Marcel. It took a long time, because we didn't have a first name or anything; but eventually we found him. And when Bill Moore (my closest associate on this investigation) visited him, he said he never heard of it, didn't know anything about it. When he went out of the room, his wife said, "He's not going to tell you anything. They've told him not to say anything." And then he gradually admitted that, well, if there *had* been a report, he would have written it, and so forth. And before Bill leaves, he brings out a copy of the book *The Roswell Incident* for Bill to sign.[10] Strange thing. I mean, he was obviously being very cautious about what he was saying. And he still won't say anything that's useful about what he did. He figures he's still under oath.

RS: But by asking for the autograph he was tacitly admitting in some sense that, yeah, you guys are doing the right research.

SF: Well, I'm not sure he was admitting that. He was admitting that he had read the book, and that contrary to his initial response, he did know about the story. People who've never had security clearances have to understand that those of us who've had security clearances *don't* casually break security, believe me we don't. And certainly, the people at Roswell at that time were not people who were casually going to break security to talk about something like this, which was probably the biggest story of the millennium: recovery of a crashed saucer *and* alien bodies outside Roswell.

RS: Okay, get to the alien bodies. How do you know that actually occurred?

SF: We have several different stories from different people. I've got a mortician whose girlfriend saw the bodies, a man who would never talk to anybody until he talked to me a year ago. His girlfriend worked at the base; she's dead, unfortunately. I have a medical technician; he saw the bodies. He hasn't gone public either, but I've talked to him. We have close associates and friends of one Barney Barnett, a civil engineer, who quietly told that when he was out in the boonies there he ran across a saucer stuck in the ground with bodies around it. The military showed up in just a few minutes, probably having tracked the object down on the radar that was at White Sands Missile Range, which is not far away. They had been scheduled for a rocket shot on July third, which didn't come off, incidentally, which was very interesting. White Sands is where all the early rocket shots were done, not far from where this thing happened.

It's interesting to speculate on why a flying saucer would go to New Mexico. In 1947, New Mexico was unique in the entire world with regard to the presence of three different areas of technology that would clearly tip off an alien visitor that, soon, Earthlings would be going to the stars. Nuclear energy: the first atom bomb test was not far from where the wreckage was recovered. Missiles: White Sands Missile Range was the only place firing major missiles in the United States at that time. And powerful radar to track the missiles. You put them all together, and suddenly, from an alien viewpoint, this planet could be a threat. It was bad enough that we were making a mess out of our own planet. We had just killed 40 million of our own during World War II. But that these guys are going to come out *our* way? You know, who needs them?

RS: How did it stay a secret for so long? There had to have been leaks. Rumors fly all over the place.

SF: Look, a press release appeared in the afternoon papers all across the country! *Afternoon* papers. But General Ramey's identification as just a weather balloon is what followed in the next morning's papers, the *New York Times, Washington Post* and so forth. They just carried the coverup.

The people were under security. The ranchers weren't part of the public. Some of the people who saw things were extraordinarily threatened; their families would be in trouble if they talked, and so forth.

Again, you need a context. This is 1947, New Mexico, where the first atom bomb had been tested just a few miles away two years before; where you have a secret city, Los Alamos, where the government presence is enormous. White Sands Missile Range is just down the road, so to speak, the biggest military base in the United States. Holloman Air Force Base is just down the road. Roswell itself still has the second largest runway in the United States. Kirtland Air Force Base is the biggest employer in the state of New Mexico. There are several other Air Force bases down there. So, the intimidation was great. As for the media, at that time there hadn't been a Watergate; they didn't think the government would lie in peacetime.

The people involved on the military side couldn't talk. Jesse Marcel was base intelligence officer. Roswell was a very busy base — I've got the base history. They were short of men, they had a big mission, the Cold War was heating up. There were things to worry about. The saucer story was curious, but that's not enough excuse to break security.

As for the other people, what's the point of talking? The government had already said it was a weather balloon. The rancher, Mac Brazel, was apparently threatened in some way and given a phony story to repeat. Some people think he was paid some money. But he never said anything more about it, even to his kids. He was intimidated. And you have to understand intimidation. These people had their lives to lead.

RS: So this ushered in the coverup. It was ad hoc at first, and then it grew upon itself. And then we have the hidden history of the post-war era that we're just beginning to find out about.

SF: You have a group of well-intentioned, very competent government people who decided that, at this point in time, there was absolutely nothing to be gained, and a great deal to lose, by announcing to the public: "There are alien invaders. We can't do anything about them, we don't know how they work, we don't know where they're from, we don't know what they want, but we thought you'd like to know." That would have been totally irresponsible for those people. I don't believe that *those* people are responsible for the ridicule that came in later.

You see, many of the people who are involved didn't have a "need to know" for knowing the facts. They thought that they were doing what they were supposed to do. Cover it up. Make fun of people. Don't let them tell the story out there.

The media were the worst of all, because they distorted what the government said. They didn't use their heads. That Project Bluebook was covering things up was perfectly obvious early on. That their rules for not having many sightings as unknowns at the end of the year were artificial, spurious and stupid was perfectly obvious, if you asked questions. But nobody asked the questions. The *Los Angeles Times* carried an editorial on *Bluebook Special Report 14* — the biggest study ever done, completed or published in 1955 but never directly released — quoting the Secretary of the Air Force: "On the basis of this report, we believe that no objects such as those popularly described as flying saucers have overflown the United States; even the unknown three percent could have been identified as conventional phenomena or illusions if more complete observational data had been available." That's what he said, and that's what appeared in all the newspapers, without ever seeing the report. The Air Force put out a summary that had *none* of the data from the 240-plus charts, tables, maps, the stuff that's in the report. They didn't even give the title of the report, and they didn't say who did the work — and nobody asked! If they had said "Bluebook Special Report 14," surely some newsman would've asked, "What do you mean, fourteen? What happened to one through thirteen?"[11] Why didn't they ask where the work was done? The *L.A. Times* editorial says, "We knew all along that this stuff was nonsense." They accepted the three percent unknowns, when in fact it was 21.5 percent. But nobody asked any of those questions or looked up any of that information. The press failed to do the job that we've accorded it in a free society.

So, you've got your government intentionally covering it up — Bluebook as a front operation, a cover operation — and the media not doing their job; and the guys on the inside could go on about their business.

RS: How do we get from there to MJ-12?

SF: There seems to have always been a conflict inside the government between those who want to release and those who don't. We know that in 1973, there was supposed to have been a series of three documentaries done about flying saucers, using only government data, each one more spectacular than the last. This was after Nixon was re-elected, so he couldn't run again and could get away with this. I talked to the people who prepared the first one, "UFOs Past, Present and Future." They didn't make the last two. They were approached by the government and had full cooperation from the government. The first show was supposed to end with some real footage of a saucer landing at Holloman Air Force Base, with aliens getting out and being greeted by military people from the base. The guy had seen the film. Other people have since come forward saying they had seen the film. And yet, that was taken away at the last minute. They hypothesized that Watergate came along. They didn't do the other two shows. But obviously there were some people who wanted to release the data.

With MJ-12, we got lucky, I guess. When Bill Moore was touting the book, *The Roswell Incident,* in 1980 and subsequently, he was approached by military intelligence insiders who showed credentials and said that they wanted to help get the information out. They weren't going public, but they'd give us some pointers. Bill and another colleague of ours, Jaime Shandera, were meeting with these insiders, and in December of 1984 a roll of 35mm film shows up at Jaime's house. No return address on the envelope. When printed, it's the first eight pages of the briefing document for President-elect Eisenhower, dated 18 November, 1952. Page eight is the Truman-Forrestal memo of September 24, 1947, authorizing Secretary of Defense Forrestal to proceed with Operation Majestic Twelve. There's a list of attachments. We only have "A," which is the Truman-Forrestal memo. We don't have "B" through "H." I'd give my left arm for those.

The question, of course, was whether the documents were legitimate, since the story they tell is spectacular; namely, that a crashed saucer was recovered outside Roswell, New Mexico, complete with four alien bodies; that they hadn't been able to decipher the strange symbols; that the "extraterrestrial biological entities" had a different biological development than us homo sapiens; that there was a contingency plan for the release of data; that they had inside contacts at Blue Book and its predecessors Sign and Grudge; and that it was strongly recommended that the group, Operation Majestic 12, be held in highest security and still accountable only to the president. There is reference made to a lot of other little details, for example, another recovered saucer near the Texas-Mexico border in 1950. So, it's a spectacular document, if it's genuine.

One of the problems is that of the twelve people listed as Majestic 12, eleven made sense, but one of them didn't: Dr. Donald Menzel, Harvard University professor of astronomy, who was a total UFO skeptic, we thought. He'd written three

anti-UFO books. Considering the level of the other people —
the first three directors of Central Intelligence, the first Secretary of Defense, people who'd been chairmen of the National
Advisory Committee on Aeronautics — what the heck was
Menzel doing on this list? How could he be part of this crew?
That was the kicker, initially; and we certainly weren't going to
go public with that. I didn't like Menzel. I thought this was
probably a phoney document. I proceeded, however, to check
things out.

To make a long story short, I determined that Menzel led
a double life. He wrote in 1960 to President Kennedy that he
had a longer continuous association with the National Security
Agency than anybody in the country, that he had a Top Secret-
Ultra clearance and had done work for the CIA. I found out he
had taught cryptography, worked in very highly classified
work during the war and maintained his close connection with
the government after the war. As a matter of fact, he had gone
through a terrible loyalty hearing in 1950, where his staunchest
defender was Dr. Vannevar Bush, who is named as one of the
wheels in MJ-12. When we finally got finished with all that, it
became more plausible that this was a genuine document.

I continued my research. I got a grant from the Fund for
UFO Research. I visited a lot of archives – fourteen over the
years, some of them many times: the Eisenhower Library, the
Truman Library, the National Archives, the Library of Congress Manuscript Division – trying to check on the documents.

There is another piece of paper that's important here,
found at the National Archive in July of 1985, roughly six or
seven months after the original MJ-12 documents. It's the only
one we have in hard copy. The others are on film, so you can't
check the paper, the ink, a lot of things. This new one was a
memo from Ike's national security advisor, Robert Cutler, to
General Nathan Twining, at that time Chief of Staff of the Air
Force. The subject was the National Security Council MJ-12
special studies project. It tells Twining that the briefing is going
to take place during the already scheduled meeting rather than
after it as originally planned. "More precise arrangements will

be explained to you upon arrival....Your concurrence in the above change of arrangements is assumed." Very brief. July 14, 1954. Top Secret, Restricted Security Information. Rather unusual labeling. It's not signed. It doesn't have a little "s" with a slash next to it either.

We've looked at the contents of the documents and whatever else we can determine about them. In the case of the Cutler-Twining memo, we have the original paper, so you can see the watermark on the onion skin with the name of the company that made the paper. We contacted them to find out when they made this particular paper, and we were told between 1953 and 1973. That's good, it covers our time period.

I was challenged by one of the noisy negativists that the type in the Cutler-Twining memo was the large pica type, while the tradition at the White House was the small elite type. They gave nine samples to prove that. Philip J. Klass, the biggest debunker in town, challenged me to provide *any* genuine memoranda or letters from the National Security Council files of that time, 1953 to '55, done in the same size and style of type as the Cutler-Twining memo. To encourage me to respond more quickly, he offered me one hundred dollars each, up to a maximum of ten (unfortunately!), for any such genuine memos. I provided him with a couple of dozen, and I got my thousand-dollar check. There's no question, in other words, that it was typed with exactly the same type-face that's used in other memos from that place and time. That doesn't prove it's genuine, but it comes closer.

I've also checked a lot of the internal information. The MJ-12 document names a thirteenth man, Walter Bedell Smith, to replace Secretary of Defense James Forrestal, who apparently committed suicide in 1949. (The medical record is still classified, incidentally.) Walter Bedell Smith was head of the CIA, succeeding Admiral Roscoe Hillenkoetter, who's named as the briefing officer for this November 18, 1952 Eisenhower briefing. It says Walter Bedell Smith became a permanent member on August 1, 1950, which, as I found out after a lot of digging, was the only date in the first ten months of that year that he met with President Truman, a short meeting at the west door of the White House, rather than the usual place, subject not disclosed. Now, how would anybody know that? The date of the Truman-Forrestal memo, September 24, 1947, was the only date when Dr. Vannevar Bush, who's named in that memo and named as part of MJ-12, met with Truman in the last eight months of 1947. He was accompanied by James Forrestal, to whom the memo is addressed, and they had met for half an hour prior to going there. The date on the memo, September 24, 1947, has a period after it, which is very peculiar indeed, except that Vannevar Bush's office always put a period after the date. I've checked with a lot of people who think there's nothing strange at all about Forrestal and Bush creating something for Truman's signature. So, there's a lot of this kind of detail. Getting back to General Twining for a minute: that strange sentence, "Your concurrence in the above change of arrangements is assumed." Earlier, in 1981, we had found two Top Secret memos in the Twining papers at the Library of Congress manuscript division, one of which had almost exactly the same language.

RS: If someone were pulling a hoax on the inside and wanted to forge a document, is it your opinion that all of these details are too numerous, too minute and too consistent to have been included in a hoax?

SF: Yes. Certainly, nobody on the outside could have done it, because nobody knows some of this stuff. It took a lot of digging in the presidential libraries and so forth to find out these things. It is conceivable that somebody went through an extraordinary amount of historical research to dig into this stuff. The trouble is, I don't see how they could have done it without spending a lot of time at the Truman and Eisenhower libraries, and we have no evidence of anybody doing that.

It's also possible that a lot of this thing is true, and that there's some phoney-baloney stuff as well. Certainly, if there wasn't an MJ-12, we'd have to invent one. They had to do something about what happened at Roswell. But that doesn't prove, even if the documents in general are correct, that the specific information is necessarily correct.

RS: What do you think of the alternate scenario put forth by Bill Cooper? He says MJ-12 didn't come into existence until 1954 under Eisenhower, that the original group is Project Sign, and that the MJ-12 document is a contingency cover.[12]

SF: I have no reason to believe what Mr. Cooper has said. It makes no sense to suggest that Sign had anything to do with what happened at Roswell.

If you look at the Twining memo to General George Schulgen,[13] dated September 23, 1947, not only does he say that these things are disk-shaped, real and so forth, the last paragraph says which groups should get copies of all the data. That includes some very interesting groups: NACA (National Advisory Committee on Aeronautics), Joint Research and Development Board, the Atomic Energy Commission, the Air Force Scientific Advisory Board, the Rand Corporation, NEPA (Nuclear Energy for Propulsion of Aircraft). These are all technical groups, and the common link in all of them is Vannevar Bush.

So, the notion that the government would have depended on Project Sign, which was a piddly operation, instead of bringing in the best and the brightest, makes no sense at all. Meanwhile, the people named to MJ-12 include Dr. Jerome Hunsaker, MIT, Chairman of NACA in 1947; and his predecessor as NACA chairman, Vannevar Bush. Detlev Bronk, an aviation physiologist — perfect guy for bodies — had headed a biology committee under Bush during the war. All the people you'd need were on that thing.

The notion that they waited until 1954 also makes no sense. Again, looking at Twining's memo, there's no question that this was being taken very seriously, as a technological problem, in 1947. So, I think Cooper is wrong about this stuff.

RS: Do you think the government is preparing us for the truth in some gradual fashion, and if so, what evidence is there that this might be taking place?

SF: It's hard to say what the government is or isn't doing. Certainly, the government is able to have an impact on the network heads and the media heads. There are people who make a big conspiracy thing about the Council on Foreign Relations and the Trilateral Commission, all the big-shots being tied in together. Maybe. I don't know. There's a story that I do know about Steven Spielberg showing *E.T.* at the White House. Reagan afterward put his hand on Spielberg's shoulder and said, "You know, there are fewer than six people in this room who know the real story." Now, that was from Spielberg to Jaime Shandera to me, and I have no reason to doubt that it's true.

You see, you can get people doing what you want them to do without demanding that they do it, without pushing, if the situation is right. If you're going to make a lot of bucks — remember, *E.T.* is the highest grossing motion picture of all time, and *Close Encounters* was high on the list before that — it wouldn't take much pushing on a guy like Spielberg to encourage him to do another UFO movie. But that doesn't mean the government paid any money into it, or anything like that.

Again, not everybody in the government knows what the government is doing, by a long shot. I do know this. I was asked by NASA, when I lived in California ten years ago, to speak to their group out at North American Rockwell, at Downey where they made the Apollo command module. They picked my brains, but they wouldn't tell me anything. I've talked to astronauts who've given every indication that they know what's going on. For example, I knew William Anders, one of the astronauts on the first mission around the moon, because we were both in radiation shielding work, compact nuclear reactors. After he became an astronaut, before that mission, we each chaired a session of a meeting of the American Nuclear Society in San Diego, and we got to talking. We spent two hours talking only about UFOs. He bought copies of everything I had with me. I asked him about the astronaut sightings, but I found out more in the Condon Report than he would tell me. It felt very much like a matter of security. I was working under clearances at the time, and so was he. I wasn't going to push him.

We know that Gordon Cooper wrote a letter to the United Nations. I've talked to Gordon about this. He says he saw UFOs flying over Germany in 1951. He thinks they're extraterrestrial spacecraft with capabilities well beyond our own. Deke Slayton has reported sighting a UFO. We know that Brian O'Leary, an astronaut who didn't fly, has made a plea for Congressional hearings on the subject of UFOs. Eugene Cernan, out of the blue at a press conference after he came back from space, said, "I've been asked, and I think these things are coming from other civilizations." I called him, just to check whether he'd really said that. He said yes, then gave me a lecture that I could have given him about not being alone in the universe. So, certainly, several of the astronauts have spoken out in a positive way.

RS: What indications, if any, do you have concerning our government's interest in your own UFO research? Have you ever felt manipulated or threatened?

SF: There are certainly indications from Bill Moore's insiders that they knew things about me that they could only have gotten by paying a great deal of attention to things I'd said at a certain closed conference in England, for example. It was clear that they knew about me and that somebody was monitoring, in other words. Bill's FBI file is 61 pages long, and they only released portions of six pages to him. What are they doing gathering data? The FBI said they have nothing on me. I pushed them, because the CIA told me all they had was a negative name-check request from the FBI with a file number. So, they rechecked. "Yes, we found a file on you. It's properly withheld under an executive order dealing with national security." I asked them what the security level was. They told me that's secret, and they wouldn't tell me how big the file was or what time-period it covered. I eventually got part of it. The government is clearly paying attention, but to just what extent, I have no idea. Nobody's ever tried to shoot me or get in my way or prevent me from saying whatever I please.

RS: Your colleague Bill Moore has publicly admitted to passing disinformation. He got up in front of the MUFON conference in Las Vegas and said, "Yes, I misled Paul Bennewitz. I reported on him to government agents."[14] How do you account for that behavior?

SF: If you read Bill's paper, what he admitted was that for a period in the early '80s, his contacts with Richard Doty at the Air Force Office of Special Investigations involved a certain amount of letting Doty know what people like Bennewitz and others knew, which wasn't much, and passing some information on to them that would be, I think, correctly called disinformation. Bill was not an agent of the government, nor did he work for the government. He cooperated, hoping that by giving something, he'd get something, which is standard practice, just as newsmen will sometimes cooperate with people in the hope of getting something useful. Now, I wasn't happy with the paper, but for other reasons. Bill should have said he was sorry if anything bad happened to Bennewitz as a result of his activities. Certainly, it was only indirectly that that was the case. He visited Bennewitz and so forth, but he didn't do anything to Bennewitz. Bennewitz wanted to believe what he wanted to believe. I'd heard two years earlier from a psychologist that he thought Bennewitz had gone off the deep end, long before Bill Moore got involved. So don't blame him for what happened to Bennewitz, if anything did.

  Bill and I differ substantially about tactics. I think he's gotten too caught up in the insiders business. As I told him, I think they've done a psychological profile on him and figured out what would make him tick, so to speak. They've dangled the carrot out in front, so that for several years he hasn't been doing anywhere near as much good research as he did on the

Roswell incident. We also disagreed about that terrible show, "UFO Cover-up Live,"[15] which I was on but was terribly disappointed in. I thought it was going to be good until I got there and wasted four days. We were reading from tele-prompters. That's not the way you do this kind of thing. When Bill stated that he thought Falcon and Condor, whose interviews he had arranged, might put out some disinformation, I found that unacceptable. If you have any reason to believe that somebody's putting out disinformation, you don't use them. I mean, it's not baseball, where if one-third of the time a guy gets a hit, he's a great player. If a guy only tells the truth one-third of the time, I don't want anything to do with him.

I still trust Bill, though I don't always know what he's doing. People have to understand, Bill was a teacher and a teacher's union negotiator for a number of years. Union negotiators have a habit of playing games, checking things out, not always being straight-forward because they want to see what the other guy's doing. It's a cagey business, and being too straight-forward means you usually get clobbered in the negotiations. Bill still has that approach to things. I'm much more straight-forward. I don't believe in playing games. It's just not my style. That's the problem with being a nuclear physicist. I'm not smart enough to play those kinds of "human" games. I deal with facts.

It is interesting that, while a number of noisy negativists have suggested that Bill faked the MJ-12 documents, not only has nobody suggested that I did it, but even the people who are noisiest against it say I'm not a candidate for the forging. Which is something, I suppose. I don't know if we'll do any more joint research. Bill and I each put out separate reports on MJ-12. And I'm working on a new book about Roswell with Don Berliner, due out in 1991.

RS: Do you accept the popular abduction scenario as valid? What do you think of Budd Hopkins' work?

SF: I don't know what the popular abduction scenario is. But I am satisfied that a number of Earthlings have, against their will, been abducted on board alien spacecraft and have been examined, treated or mistreated, and put back out, and often told they wouldn't remember; and that they didn't remember until regressive hypnosis. Now, there are a lot of variations on that theme; for example, cases of ova or sperm being taken, and so forth. It's very hard to give one straight-forward presentation as to what happens during an abduction. Fortunately, Dr. Eddie Bullard of Indiana University has done a huge study of hundreds of abductions and finds there's a great consistency in the stories.[16]

I think a great deal of Budd Hopkins' work, partly because he's used a lot of professional psychologists and psychiatrists with him, and because I find Budd to be a caring person. But he's not the only researcher, of course. Dr. James Harder has worked with 200 abductees, Dr. Leo Sprinkle has worked with a couple of hundred, Dr. Richard Haines has worked with some. There's a whole bunch more.

Budd has intentionally withheld certain specific details from abduction accounts, so that if he comes across them in the next story, he knows they didn't come from his books or his public discussions; and these little details have repeatedly turned up. Then there was a little experiment done up in Canada. Five professionals were given samples of what were supposedly drawings of writing seen on board flying saucers by five abductees, none of the abductees having seen the other drawings. And these five professionals agreed without hesitation that these five abductees clearly were reporting the same thing. That's hard to explain as coincidence, when you figure all the forms that writing can take.

So, yes, there are a lot of abductions going on, even as we speak, I guess. I have to be careful here. I'm not saying that everybody who claims to have been abducted has been abducted. That's not the question. Have *some* Earthlings been abducted by aliens? Yes.

RS: Then you have the claims from people like Whitley Strieber that there are all these other dimensions to it, all the personal and spiritual and psychological dimensions, and that we may not be dealing with extraterrestrials, we may be dealing with inter-dimensional beings or beings from the future, even our own descendants coming back to sculpt time. There have been all kinds of suggestions. You seem to take a very specific interpretation that we're dealing with extraterrestrials. Is there a conflict of point of view?

SF: I don't think there's a conflict. There's a different approach. Again, if an alien spaceship gets here by warping space and time, I suppose you can call that moving through dimensions. That doesn't change that it's an extraterrestrial spaceship. I'm not even ruling out movement in time. We do that with the space telescope. If you watch something 13 billion light years away, you're moving in time.

   With Whitley, I think, you have to recognize that he's a very imaginative writer, and was long before *Communion*.[17] He's not a UFO expert by any means. He certainly can think up scenarios, probably 20 times as many as I could, because he's a science-fiction type of writer and he's a very bright guy. But just because he can think up a scenario doesn't mean that's reality. You could say that the reason the moon only shows in crescent form part of the month is that the earth's shadow is blotting out the rest of the moon. That's a plausible explanation, but it's the wrong explanation, except during an eclipse. So, because it's plausible doesn't mean it's right.

   I work on evidence, the other way around. I don't reach a conclusion about something until I have the evidence. There are certainly aspects of the abduction phenomenon, the UFO phenomenon, which I can't explain and don't understand. I'd be astonished if there weren't. How could it be that somebody could be way ahead of us and not know things that we don't know? To me, that only makes sense. And when you consider the time available — the universe is about 15 billion years old. Our lifespan, our history of technology, is awfully small, and look how it's changed in the last fifty years. So, I'm not bothered, I'm intrigued by what some people might think of as inconsistencies and unexplained phenomena. It's uproarious that anybody would think we should be able to explain everything about these guys.

RS: Recently we've had several apparent "breakthroughs," like Bob Lazar, MJ-12, Gulf Breeze. It seems like all hell is breaking loose, but what are we to make of it all, really?

SF: I've had one telephone conversation with Bob Lazar. I've tried to check on him. That was my first response when I heard about him. Who is this guy, what's his background, what can we find out? I checked the American Physical Society, and there's nobody by that name listed. I checked MIT, Caltech and Cal State Northridge, and none of them have ever heard of him. I checked Pierce College. He did attend an electronics course back before 1977, which hardly makes him a far-out physicist.

There is certainly classified work going on at Groom Lake, Area 51, Nellis Air Force Base and all these places around Las Vegas. And there are certainly underground bases there. You've got to hide from the Soviet overflights. Satellites go over there every day, maybe every couple of hours. So that part of his story is OK.

I've listened to Bob on tape, and I'm impressed that he's a sharp guy. I have no way to justify saying yea or nay to his notions about element 115, matter-antimatter and all the other stuff that he talks about. The thing is, we don't even have a gram of element 115. We do make anti-matter in various accelerators. But Bob said nothing that would give me a real handle on checking. That's good and bad at the same time. If he were indeed doing what he said he's been doing, you'd expect him to know something the rest of us don't know. I've heard nothing that would immediately say to me that he's not a physicist.

But I'm bothered when I can't check somebody out, frankly, because a professional person should leave a trail. He was supposed to send me his resume, and I've been waiting. I haven't received anything from him. Some people claim that he's a fraud, but I won't say that yet. He's in my gray basket too.

MJ-12 is an ongoing thing. I'm disgusted at the level of some of the attacks that are made on it by people who don't know what they're talking about, who pretend they're experts but have never even been to an archive. I find that almost laughable.

Gulf Breeze, on the other hand, is a fait accompli now. I'm satisfied that the Gulf Breeze story as told by Ed Walters in his book is legitimate [see Briefing, next page]. I base that not only on meeting Ed and his wife Frances, but also on a lot of hours with Bruce Maccabee, going over his analysis of the photos and videotape; and talking with Budd Hopkins, who spent a lot of time in Gulf Breeze meeting with Ed and Frances and their neighbors. It's not just a quicky conclusion.

Bruce Maccabee is an extraordinarily careful and competent researcher. He's an optical physicist, works for a government lab, and is also Chairman of the Fund for UFO Research. I've known him for a lot of years and would trust him on anything. Bruce showed me, especially with the stereo pictures that were taken, how it was impossible to fake those things, practically speaking. How do you fake a picture? You've got to have a small model. That's easy enough. But to get a good stereo picture at some distance, I just can't imagine somebody running around throwing big, eight-foot saucers into the sky and managing to successfully photograph them.

The critics have been nasty and irrational. For example, the craft pictured in most of Ed's photos doesn't look like they think a flying saucer should look. Well, who knows what it should look like? A Volkswagen doesn't look like a Rolls Royce, but so what? That doesn't mean either one is phoney. Remember, one of the most important aspects of Ed's case is that there were so many other people in the community who said, when they saw the pictures, "That's what I saw." You can fool some of the people some of the time, but when you get over a hundred witnesses, that's really reaching. You're making this guy a special guru if you think he can tell all these people to lie

BRIEFING:

Close Encounters in Gulf Breeze

Gulf Breeze is a quiet, affluent seacoast community near Pensacola on the Florida panhandle. On November 19, 1987, the weekly *Gulf Breeze Sentinel* published two photos of a UFO on page one, accompanied by a letter from "Mr. X" explaining that he had taken the photos on November 11 from the front yard of his house and wondered if anyone else had seen what he saw. Thus began one of the most impressive multiple-sighting cases in UFO history.

Mr. X turned out to be Ed Walters, a successful building contractor liked and trusted by his neighbors and well-known for his civic activities. Between November 11, 1987 and May 1, 1988, Ed took 39 UFO photographs during 20 separate sighting episodes. Most of his photos showed clear details of a round, domed object with a bright ring of light on its lower surface. Several of his photos were taken with a self-referencing stereo camera that permitted expert photo analysts to determine that the object was both too large and too far away to be a model. Many other analytic tests also supported the claim that Ed's photos were authentic. The object had the appearance of an unconventional aircraft unlike anything of human manufacture.

Ed's wife Frances and their two teenage children were also witnesses, along with over 100 other residents of Gulf Breeze. Photos of similar UFOs were taken by others as well, including "Believer Bill" and "Jane," whose photos were published along with many of Ed's in *The Gulf Breeze Sightings* by Ed and Frances Walters (Morrow, 1990). In the book, Ed also revealed that he had been abducted and had many times experienced apparent telepathic contact with an intelligence behind the UFOs. His testimony has been augmented by four successful polygraph tests and hypnotic regression.

Abduction expert Budd Hopkins, photo expert Bruce Maccabee and MUFON Director Walter Andrus, among others, have publicly endorsed Ed Walters' claims. Nonetheless, the case has attracted debunkers and aroused controversy among UFO researchers. The Center for UFO Studies in Chicago, one of America's most respected UFO research organizations, has denounced the case as a fraud.

In June, 1990, a Gulf Breeze resident living in a house formerly owned by Ed Walters brought forth a paper and styrofoam model closely resembling the object in many of Ed's photos. The model, it was claimed, was found in the attic of the house. At the same time, a 22-year-old man who at first used the name "Chris" came forward saying he knew that Ed had faked the photos. "Chris," who was later identified as Tommy Smith, showed as evidence six other photos, very similar to Ed's, that he said were fakes. Oddly, photo expert Bruce Macabbee later examined these photos and said they appeared to be authentic. Similarly, Donald Ware [see Chapter Six] said he had learned months earlier that a young man had taken several such photos of a UFO like that seen by Ed Walters but had feared to disclose them, possibly for religious reasons.

In the wake of this controversy, Ed Walters underwent and passed his fourth polygraph test, which dealt specifically with the allegations of fraud. The model, he said, was made in September of 1989 or later, because the paper used in its construction contained a sketch on its inside surface that he drew at that time. He surmised that the paper was taken from his trash and used in the model in an effort to debunk his claims. Meanwhile, no one connected with the investigation seems able to account for the accusations of Tommy Smith. The controversy continues.[18] –ML

on his behalf. That's unreasonable.

RS: We have a very extraordinary situation here. I interviewed Ed Walters recently, and he said, quote, "As we speak, it's still going on. I haven't seen some for a while, but just a week ago, out of the police station, there was a sighting. People are seeing these things every single day. The case is ongoing." My question to you, Stanton Friedman, nuclear physicist, is: Why isn't the National Academy of Sciences out there at Gulf Breeze, Florida?

SF: The National Academy of Sciences has never shown much imagination about flying saucers. The forward they wrote for the Condon Report, for example, was an atrocious piece of work by a group of outstanding scientists who obviously didn't know anything about flying saucers. They investigated no cases, they read none of the evidence, they simply took one of their own on face value. Since they endorsed Condon, they certainly can't change their endorsement. Ed Condon was a member of the National Academy of Sciences. So was Donald Menzel, who had put out all those anti-UFO books. So, the National Academy of Sciences only does what it gets asked to do. It is not an initiator, it's a responder, generally speaking.

RS: Assuming the evidence known to you establishes beyond a reasonable doubt that some UFOs are alien spacecraft, can you venture some speculation on why the American public seems so blase about the biggest story of the millennium?

SF: Obviously, if the journalists and network news commentators were vying with each other for the latest UFO story, things would change very quickly. But I can give four major reasons why the big-shots of science and journalism haven't jumped on the pro-UFO bandwagon:

1) ignorance of the relevant data;

2) the "laughter curtain," or fear of ridicule;

3) ego: "If aliens were coming here, they'd want to talk to me. They haven't asked for an appointment, so they must not be coming here;" and

4) a total unwillingness to use our knowledge of technology to understand the behavior of the flying saucer: "You can't get here from there, you can't move like that," and all the other nonsense. Every generation thinks it knows everything there is to know.

These four reasons have coupled to keep the media and the scientific community away. And if you keep them away, who's left? Not many. Who has the resources? When I was working on nuclear airplanes at the end of the 1950s, we were spending 100 million dollars a year — 3,500 people full-time, eleven hundred professionals. That's a lot of effort. So I know how much it costs to do a good technical job. I had contracts to do some intelligence-type work, evaluating Soviet technology with regard to compact reactors for space applications. I spent a lot of money. I did it full-time for a couple of years to come up with two reports. So, you can't do the really good work without some funding. That's the major stumbling block.

I'm glad for the Ed Walters of the world, because that gives a human dimension to what's going on. I'm much more concerned about what's happening on the inside, government level, and the future of our planet. I can't believe that this isn't going to have an impact on it.

RS: There are rumors flying around that what we're dealing with are malevolent beings. Their behavior is frightening and sometimes seems cruel, if you take numerous abduction accounts at face value. So, how are we to take this? Maybe this is part of why it's being hidden from us. What do you think?

SF: You've got both possibilities. Certainly, there are aspects of alien behavior that are distressing, when you have an ovum taken from you, when you're taken against your will from your bed or your car at somebody else's beck and call. That's demeaning. It certainly doesn't seem we're being treated as equals. We probably aren't equals, for that matter. That doesn't mean malevolence, however.

Most Americans seem to want to think of the aliens as either good guys or bad guys. They can't allow for the in-between, neutral guy doing his job. The graduate student doing his thesis research, the intelligence agent collecting data, maybe the genetics guy trying to manufacture the right combination of ingredients. My reading of the situation is that we're dealing with neutrals who don't want to be bothered. They will respond in self-defense, and will treat us sort of as we treat dumb animals.

We go out into the Arctic boonies and shoot a dart gun into a baby polar bear. He doesn't know what the heck is going on. Then we attach a radio transmitter that's going to send a signal to a satellite and back to the lab a thousand miles away. He *certainly* doesn't know what's going on! And he may be uncomfortable, because when the dart hits him, it hurts, and he falls over and hits his head. Then he goes back and talks to his friends. "Boy, do I have a headache." "What happened?" "Well, I don't know. There were these strange little guys out there, and they moved something toward me, and the next thing I know, I'm waking up and they're not around." "Come on, that's a crazy story," say the other bears. Would you say we were being cruel to him? No. Did he like what was happening to him? No.

It appears that a number of beings from elsewhere have a

project that involves abducting lots of Earthlings, whether the Earthlings like it or not. That's not nice, but certainly it isn't "Shoot first, ask questions later," which is what we seem to do. I think there is disinformation about the malevolency. I think some of the government manipulation of the information is a large-scale psychological study on how people react.

We're dealing with a huge story here, involving lots of people that we haven't heard about, involving what you might describe as treachery on the part of aliens, and treachery on the part of Earthlings. I happen to think it's an extraordinarily important story, whether these are good guys or bad guys, partly because I believe aliens think of us as a primitive society whose major activity is tribal warfare. Our record is pretty darn bad. Forty million of our own killed in World War Two, an equal number since then, needlessly. As we speak, today, there will be more than 35,000 children dying around the planet needlessly, from an absence of medicine or food. This is a strange society. I think that every new frontier for us has been a new place to do battle. That's a terrible comment on us.

I'm an optimist, in that I think an Earthling orientation will move toward solutions to all these problems. The easiest way to get that is to recognize that somebody's coming here, and to those aliens, we are all Earthlings. My hope, my bottom line if you will, is that perhaps my children's generation will create a planet sufficiently advanced over where we are now that we can qualify for admission to what I call the Cosmic Kindergarten, and that the next generation can indeed provide a planet that is suitable for intelligent life. I don't think we've managed that so far.

Chapter Two
Linda Moulton Howe:
The "Alien Harvest" and Beyond

Linda Moulton Howe is a professional filmmaker with a Masters
Degree in communications from Stanford University. She has
devoted her film and television career to documentary and
studio productions concerning science, medicine and the environment. She is the recipient of local, national and international
awards, including three regional Emmies for her documentaries. One Emmy honored her 1980 production, *A Strange Harvest*, which explored the animal mutilation phenomenon prevalent throughout the United States, Canada, Latin America and
parts of Europe since 1967. This powerful film included evidence that numerous cases of animal mutilation might be
linked to alien activity.

In 1989, Linda produced a synthesis of her last ten years
of research and personal experience concerning the alien presence in a book entitled *An Alien Harvest: Further Evidence
Linking Animal Mutilation and Human Abduction to Alien Life
Forms*. In 1990, she produced a two-hour television special,
"Earth Mysteries: Alien Life Forms," in association with WATL/
FOX 36 in Atlanta, Georgia. During the same period, she also
worked as Director of International Programming for the environmental series, "Earthbeat," on Ted Turner's WTBS Super-
station in Atlanta, and produced a variety of other television
programming. Linda thus stands as a pioneer in the difficult
business of maintaining a successful media career while pursu-
ing the hard facts on alien activity.

I first met Linda in May, 1990 in San Diego, where she was
speaking on her alien-related research at a conference. Since
then, we have shared insights on every aspect of the alien
presence. I greatly value her ongoing contributions as a researcher and educator, as well as her friendship.

Linda's video, *A Strange Harvest*, and her book, *An Alien Harvest*, can be ordered directly from her. For further information, write to LMH Productions, P.O. Box 538, Huntingdon Valley, PA 19006-0538; or call 215-938-7869.

My associate Ralph Steiner conducted the following interview with Linda in June of 1990. — ML

Linda Moulton Howe

Ralph Steiner: What's the connection between the animal mutilation phenomenon and UFOs?

Linda Howe: It goes back to September of 1967, when an Appaloosa mare called Lady was found dead and stripped of flesh from the neck up on a ranch near Mount Blanca in the San Luis Valley of Colorado. The story of Lady's death made world-wide headlines and was probably the first global public attention to the phenomenon that has come to be known as animal mutilation. Now, why the connection to UFOs?

In that summer of 1967, there had been many reports of strange lights and very odd, zooming little craft in that valley. The Sangre de Cristo mountains are in an area where even the Indians have legends about strange objects and lights flying in and out of the mountains. Besides all these strange lights in the sky, there was also a medical doctor who went to the scene of Lady's death. Unbeknown to anyone, he took some tissue samples from that horse back to Denver, analyzed them under a microscope and concluded that whatever had made the cuts in this horse had done so with high heat. It was as if the cuts were cauterized. But in 1967, we did not have lasers in surgical apparatus, so the doctor was very puzzled by the evidence of heat, a kind of darkened, hard edge to the cuts. He was also puzzled by the fact that all of the organs inside the chest area known as the mediasternum had been removed very cleanly. And to his astonishment, there was no sign of blood anywhere in the chest, on the hair, or on the ground. I would say that this lack of blood in the cases that I and others have investigated right from the beginning has been one of the hallmarks of the animal mutilation mystery.

Overall, the strange characteristics of these mutilations suggest that human technology is not involved, and natural causes definitely can't account for it, so that begs the question, How does it occur? Alien activity has to be considered.

RS: Some people say these mutilations go back even to the last century on the Great Plains of the United States. What can you say about that?

LH: I've heard stories like everyone else, but in terms of actual facts, photographs, veterinarian reports and newspaper reports, my files start in 1967. They go up into Canada in the late 1960s and early '70s. There were numerous reports in the Great Lakes area of the United States and Canada, so many that *Newsweek* magazine in 1974 ran an article about this strange mystery.[1] By 1975-76, the number of mutilations had increased to such a point that some sheriffs were getting three or four calls a day. They were getting to carcasses that were still warm to the touch, with these strange, bloodless cookie-cutter cuts very cleanly excising an ear, an eye, the jaw stripped of flesh similar to the horse, the tongue removed deep within the throat, the sexual organs — male or female — cleanly cut away, and the rectum cored out. Typically, too, there were no tracks around the animal, not even the animal's own tracks. That was the standard pattern of mutilations over the last quarter of a century. But whatever had happened prior to 1967 in other parts of the country or the world, I don't have in my files.

Q: What makes 1967 such a remarkable year?

LH: Well, none of us knows. Why is there a seeming cycle or pattern to some of these events? In the UFO phenomenon, there have been what are referred to as flaps, years in which there has been intense UFO activity. That included the 1940s in the Southwest; and 1952-54, when UFOs were recorded and sighted over Washington, DC. The 1961-67 period was another flap, and that included the famous Betty and Barney Hill abduction story, which was the first abduction to be made public. 1973 was another big year for both UFOs and human abductions, and I would say that mutilations were getting off to a start by then in a broader way.

There seemed to be cycles of everything happening in the two years 1975-76. There were mutilations that were associated with very large, football field-sized orange glowing craft over some pastures, associated with beams of light in other pastures, along with eye-witness accounts of strange non-human creatures where mutilations were found. There were mysterious dark helicopters — whether they are our government's, trying to investigate what the alien life-forms are doing, or alien craft somehow disguised as helicopters, I don't know. There were all kinds of Bigfoot sightings: large, six to eight-foot hairy creatures sighted on ranches and in areas where the animal mutilations were being found, as well as in areas where the lights were being seen. There were also a lot of human abductions during that period of time. The acceleration in those two years was as if something out there had some need, or was anticipating some need.

But there has never been a year since 1967 when mutilations have not been reported, so it's not as if they got what they needed and went away. There's been a general tapering in the number of reports, but again, there've been years such as 1979 where there was an increase in mutilations. They continued pretty steadily in 1980, then were a little quieter until 1984, when there were a lot of mutilations again. There were fewer in 1985-86, and more in 1987-88. Last year [1989], I would say, there was a general increase again. So far in 1990, there have been reports from North Carolina and Kentucky, from Canada, and sheep mutilations in England — so the reports continue as we speak.

RS: You're saying it's a global phenomenon, not just here in the United States?

LH: It has been global right from the beginning. After that horse was found in Colorado, the reports in Canada began, and there are reports from the 1970s out of Australia, the Canary Islands off the coast of Africa, parts of Europe, South America, Central America, Mexico, Puerto Rico. This is a worldwide phenomenon, not confined to the United States.

RS: Some people, in attempting to explain the phenomenon in prosaic terms, have singled out the possibility that Satanic cults might be roaming the Southwest of the United States, performing strange rituals on cattle. Some people have actually said that they have identified some groups that might be involved in the activity. Do you have any evidence of that?

LH: Right in the beginning of my work on the documentary film, *A Strange Harvest*, I went to see a man named Carl Whiteside. He was the Chief Investigator of Animal Mutilations in Colorado, and he was one of the directors of the Colorado Bureau of Investigation. We went through the list of possibilities of what was behind the mutilations, and we started with predators. That was easily dismissed in many cases, because necropsy reports had established that the cuts were made with something sharp. As for Satanic cults, he said there were undercover agents from Colorado to California trying to come up with a shred of evidence about a Satanic cult connection to mutilations, and they have never come up with anything. Furthermore, he said, this was the first time in his law enforcement career that they had posted a large reward, asking for any information concerning the animal mutilations, and they never had one person come forward to even claim information. So, in terms of Colorado's perspective on a Satanic cult connection, they turned up zero.

After *A Strange Harvest* was broadcast in May of 1980, I received a call from the Royal Canadian Mounted Police. A man there named Lynn Lauber was investigating a series of mutilations they were having, and he was aware that my documentary found a strong connection between alien life form activity and mutilations. He told me on the phone that they were trying to make a connection to a Satanic cult up there, but he would like to see my film. I sent it to him. Later on, when we again talked privately on the phone, it was very clear to me that, in spite of public reports in the Canadian newspapers that the mutilations were tied to Satanic cults, the Royal Canadian Mounted Police investigator did not have strong enough evidence to link to Satanic cults. In fact, he definitely left open the possibility of a link between mutilations and UFOs.

RS: Has anybody been able to obtain photographic evidence of a mutilation occurring? It seems that if the phenomenon is as widespread as you claim, there must be some way to take a picture of this.

LH: In the 1970s, there were so many mutilations that ranchers carried rifles and shot at helicopters. They formed their own private vigilante groups in at least two cases, one in Montana and one in Colorado. Men with rifles ringed pastures where there had been repetitive mutilations. In one case, the sheriff and deputies were there with the ranchers throughout an entire night. When they left, just as the sky was getting light, the sheriff went back to his office downtown to drop off some things before he went home to get some rest. As soon as he got to the office, the phone rang, and it was the amazed rancher saying, "You won't believe this, but there's a mutilation right in the middle of the pasture that we watched all night." That happened more than once.

Whatever the phenomenon is, it is able to cloak itself. There was a woman in eastern Colorado who told me that one night out on her deck, she heard a helicopter coming toward her house, and she scanned the sky hard looking for it. The noise came as if it were right on top of her roof. She said the noise was so loud it scared her little dog, who went barking into the bedroom, and yet there was nothing in the sky. She could never see anything, but she heard this loud noise. That combination of events was reported by many people, hearing something that sounded like a plane or a helicopter, but not seeing anything — again, some strange aberration, a cloaking device perhaps.

In January, 1990, a man named Marty Gilbert, who works as a stringer for a TV station in Louisville, Kentucky, was out doing a music video on a farm, and he saw trees about two blocks away move as if the wind were blowing in them. It puzzled him, because where he was the air was very still. He also thought that he saw something move in the trees. Finally, his curiosity got the best of him, and he moved with his camera the two blocks to the trees. I have a videotape of what he found when he walked in there rolling his camera. It's a six-month-old male calf, a steer. The bottom half of the calf had been removed in what looks like a circular saw excision. The eye exposed to the air had turned a milky blue-white, another phenomenon that had been seen in mutilations over the last twenty years. One medical doctor told me that eye tissue exposed to high heat or radiation will turn this blue-white color. There was no blood anywhere on the ground, nor on the hair of the calf. Yet, Marty Gilbert said that as he walked up, there was steam rising from the body of this calf in the cold air. Whatever had happened was that fresh. Now, what could possibly have removed the back half of this calf and literally scorched the eye to a blue-white, leaving the body still steaming as Marty comes in with his camera, but not a sign of blood anywhere? What was there? No object was seen or heard, outside of Marty seeing that the trees were moving as if there were wind in them.

RS: I know that there have been some photographs of lights doing maneuvers in the sky, and there are also reports of unmarked helicopters that you mentioned previously. Has there been any attempt to track down whether the helicopters are involved with the mutilation?

LH: In the 1970s, when the dark, silent helicopters were most intensely reported, there were a lot of people trying to make a connection between the helicopters and the mutilations. I talked to Lou Girodo, who was the chief investigator on mutilations in the DA's office in Trinidad, Colorado throughout the 1970s. One night in his office in October of 1979, with my film camera running, I asked him about the helicopters, and this was his answer. He said they had so many reports of completely silent helicopters that he had come to the conclusion that they were dealing with something not from this planet. These were his words: "creatures not from this planet." One of the possibilities for these silent, strange helicopters was that this life-form had some kind of technology to camouflage themselves however they wanted to, and in some cases chose to look like a helicopter that didn't make any noise. Now, that was a law enforcement officer's perspective after several years of investigating mutilations.

RS: Is there any indication that humans are being mutilated in the same way as cattle and sheep?

LH: It's a very difficult subject, because no one wants that to be a fact. I and others have received reports about human mutilations that match identically the excisions on the animals. However, I never have received an autopsy report with photographs that would meet the criteria for information that I would report publicly. For example, in the mutilations that I deal with publicly, I always have a sheriff's report and photographs, and often the rancher's report, and as many times as I can, the veterinarian report, so that I have a full and complete case. The human mutilations have been reported by military people and by law enforcement. What the exact facts are, I don't know, and I find that it is a very troubling area to try to deal with publicly.

RS: Do you see any correlations between human abductions and animal mutilations?

LH: Yes. I think the most important and definite parallel between the animal mutilations and the human abductions is this. In the human abduction cases, pieces of tissue from various parts of the body are often taken. In women, there are often reports of vaginal exams of some sort, and the removal of ova or eggs from the ovaries. In men, it is common to have a description that sperm is somehow removed. In both cases, you have a focus on the reproductive organs. Often, too, we hear about the excision of skin from legs, from hips, from the stomach, the chest and other areas. In some cases, humans report that something is inserted in their nose, their eye, their ear or some other part of their body, which is often considered to be some sort of a monitoring device, or may be for some other purpose that is unknown to the humans.

When you go over to the animal mutilations, you've got a parallel in the sense that tissue is excised. Great quantities of fluid are removed. The genital areas are taken, for the most part. There's a parallel there, but the difference is that the animals are returned to pastures dead and mutilated, while humans for the most part are returned with these odd excisions, or burns, or various things done to their bodies; but they are alive.

RS: The question is, who's doing it? Are there any general descriptions that run throughout the experiences, both for the cattle mutilators and the human abductors?

LH: It would appear that one particular type comes up the most, and that is the one referred to as the small "Gray," with the large eyes and four fingers with sort of claws at the end. I think this is well represented in the Judy Doraty case, which I focused on in *A Strange Harvest*.

This case began in May, 1973, outside of Houston. Judy Doraty and her family had been out playing bingo one night and were headed home. Five of them were in a car when they saw a strange, bright light in the sky and began arguing about what it was. The brother-in-law insisted that it was simply a helicopter. Judy Doraty pulled over to the side of the road, got out of the car, and saw this light circle down toward a pasture near where she had stopped. Then, as far as her conscious memory was concerned, she got back in the car not feeling well, feeling very thirsty and nauseous. Everyone in the car spoke up again, asking if she had seen anything closer in the light. She told them that it had simply circled over her, and they drove home.

After that experience, she started having terrible headaches. Finally, after five years, she went to a doctor. The doctor did hypnosis, and out came this remarkable story that at the moment when she stepped out of the car and went around to the rear, she and the other people in the car became victims of what is known as missing time. Somehow, everyone else was put in suspended animation, and some part of Judy was apparently lifted or transported into this ring of lights. But before she was lifted into whatever this was, she saw a pale yellow beam of light come down from the ring of lights into the pasture, and she saw a calf going up through this beam of light. The next thing she knew, she was inside the craft.

During her first hypnosis session in 1978, however, Judy

only recalled parts of her experience. I heard a tape of this session and decided Judy might be able to shed light on the possible alien connection with mutilations. In March of 1980, I helped arrange for her to do another hypnosis session with Dr. Leo Sprinkle, which brought out more detail.[2]

Judy told Dr. Sprinkle that once she got inside the craft, she found herself watching as parts of the calf were excised. Its tongue was removed, as apparently were the testicles and an eye. Tubes were inserted in these various organs, and small slices were made. She generally described a very medical, scientific laboratory scene in which this calf was the focus of all the cutting and probing. Finally, Dr. Sprinkle asked, "Is there anyone with you?" There was a very long pause, and she said, "I feel the presence of other things, but I can't see them," as if she had a mental block. A little later in the session, she got through the block and said that there were two little men. She drew a face very similar to the face now so widely distributed on the cover of Whitley Strieber's book, *Communion*, with the large eyes and the very narrow chin. But the difference in the Judy Doraty case was that the eyes had verticle slits like a cat or a crocodile. In other cases, such as Strieber's, the eyes are described as being large, slanted and solid black. What the relationship is between these different kinds of Grays, as they're called, with their different eyes, is a puzzle to everyone I know. One possibility is that the solid black could represent a kind of eye-covering.

In 1980, outside of Waco, Texas, there was a rancher who was trying to round up some pregnant cows in a ravine. He'd gotten all the cows but one, and he wanted that last cow. He was climbing up around some mesquite trees on a little hill, when he encountered what he said were two creatures, "the color of mesquite leaves in the spring," which is kind of a grayish-chartreuse. They had very large, egg-shaped heads with the pointed end down, and long, solid black eyes slanted up along-side the head. The rancher said they were about four feet tall, and that they were all the same color, from the top of their heads to the bottom of their feet. He didn't know if he was looking at hide, skin, or some kind of body stocking on them. And in between these two creatures, they were carrying a calf.

That rancher was petrified. He ran away, and it took him three days to get up the courage to go back. When he did, he took his wife and his son with him back to that location. There they found the calf, completely eviscerated of skeleton and organs. The hide had been turned inside out and folded very neatly on the ground so that the head and the four hooves were together, underneath the turned inside-out skin. Lying next to it was the backbone of the calf, minus every rib. The rancher said to me, "Who would do this, and what are they trying to tell us?" Those are the same two questions that I've heard from law enforcement since I got into this story ten years ago.

RS: Considering the controversy on the motives of the so-called Grays, what do you think their agenda is on earth and with us?

LH: From the few confidential sources that have come to me in the past four years, including people with military background and, in some cases, intelligence or government background, the same general storyline emerges. One of these Gray groups has some kind of a survival problem, and at least one of the reasons for the animal mutilations is to gather enough fluid, I guess from the hemoglobin and the plasma, to make some kind of essential bio-chemical ingredient that these creatures need. And every time I've said that publicly, people always come back with a very good question. If we are dealing with an alien life form that is sophisticated enough to travel in these silver disks across who knows how many light years to get here, then why is it that they would need to harvest tissues and fluid from earth life? There is something about it all that does not seem logical to humans. But then again, how can we second-guess an alien life form's problems or needs?

That may be part of the story. I don't know that it's all of the story. Another reason for the harvest that has been given by various sources is that we are dealing with alien life forms who are doing genetic experiments here with our DNA, meaning that the chromosomal material extracted from human abductees and from the animals is somehow being used to construct, perhaps, some other kind of life form. Whether or not this genetic experimentation is taking place on the earth or some place else in the galaxy, I don't know, and I don't know anyone who has an answer. There are rumors about underground bases in the United States and other parts of the world where at least some faction of these Grays work and live, but I personally have yet to see anything I feel constitutes hard proof for such a statement. What other reasons could there be besides genetic experimentation and sustenance? I don't know.

RS: There are rumors of other entities visiting the earth as well. Could you describe if there's any firm evidence of alien races visiting earth apart from the Grays, and if so, what do you think their agenda may be in relationship to the human race as well as in relationship to the Grays?

LH: One of the most provocative cases to me personally is one that has just surfaced in the past few months, due to the work of a psychologist in Missouri with whom I'm in contact. The case involves a husband and wife who, in July of 1983, watched from their porch on their farm, through binoculars, while two small, very white-skinned, very large-headed beings, not humans but they didn't know what to call them — little entities in very shiny silver leotard-like suits — had a cow down on the ground in the pasture. They were running their hands above the cow in some odd fashion. The couple both had the impression that this cow was alive. Its eyes were open. They had no idea what these little creatures were doing to it. And through binoculars they could see, some feet away, a taller being that the woman, I think, called a "lizard-guy." The description of the husband and wife is the same, that this humanoid creature stands about six feet tall, has greenish skin, scaly like a reptile or a lizard, with very large, pale green eyes with vertical slit pupils — here comes the vertical slit pupil again. Both the husband and wife could see this creature staring straight back at them in the binoculars. The wife said that she could see the little white beings do something with their hands, and this cow seemed to rise up a bit in the pasture and, for lack of a better word, *floated* with them into some kind of a silver object that the husband said reminded him of an upside-down ice cream cone — I assume that means conical and somewhat pointed. Then they all disappeared.

Now, this lizard type has been described in a few other abduction cases, although not many. Some people have tried to suggest that these lizard people are the actual brains behind the little Grays. And yet, in the hypnosis session that the psychologist later did with the Missouri woman, about another incident in their area in which she appears to have been abducted, the lizard creature that she recognized from the pasture was apparently on this craft, or wherever it was that they were giving her a vaginal exam. There were also the small, white-skinned, large-eyed Grays. They were both together in the same room handling this Missouri woman, and the psychologist asked her who seemed to be in charge. Without any hesitation, she said the little guys. Then the psychologist said that on this planet, we usually assume that people who are tall are the ones in charge. She came back immediately and said, "Oh no, the little guys are the boss." That is one abductee's perception about the little Grays and these tall lizard-looking ones.[3]

Then there was the Travis Walton encounter in 1975, in Snowflake, Arizona. Travis Walton was on a logging truck with several other guys, and they saw a white, glowing craft-like thing come down into the forest. Travis jumped out of the truck, ran out underneath the craft, and a beam of light hit him in the chest. He zonked out, and his buddies in the truck got scared, hit the accelerator and drove away. Travis Walton was not returned for five days. It's one of the longest abduction cases on record. In his particular case, after the hypnosis work was done with him, he described first encountering the very white-skinned, very large-headed Grays with large black eyes. But he tried to hit them with something; he tried to fight them, and he was paralyzed. Then they left the room, and he wandered around the craft. Suddenly, there appeared what he first thought were NASA astronauts. He was so happy to see them that he wanted to grab ahold of them, but then he realized they had glass bubbles on their heads. Their hair was a yellowish sandy color, almost down to their shoulders, and their eyes were yellow. They were wearing blue, tight-fitting uniforms, and they made no communication with him: no talking, no telepathy, nothing. So, here is a case in which these blond human-looking ones were in the same craft or area with the white-skinned, black-eyed Grays. No one seems to understand the connection between these two, including Travis Walton.[4]

RS: What, if anything, do you think justifies the government's behavior regarding the alien presence, and how ready do you think the American people are to learn the truth?

LH: I think everybody in the 1990s is very eager to know the truth. I think there is a general grass-roots suspicion that we are not being dealt with by the government in a forthright way, and that much is suppressed. Many people, I think, are even getting past being jaded and cynical about it, and are feeling distrust and in some cases very nervous about what information is being withheld.

Now, why would the United States government or other governments have chosen a policy of silence about something as historically significant as contact with another intelligence from someplace else in the universe? I wasn't there in the 1930s and '40s, but when I piece together some of the things I've learned, the picture looks like this. In spite of most of the public information which says that the first contact with some sort of alien was in the crash at Roswell in July of 1947, I and others have received information that suggests that our government was dealing with alien life forms going back at least to the early 1940s and perhaps the late '30s. Truman was dealing with a vicious and horrible war, and one of the biggest worries that the Allies had was what kind of technology the Germans might have that could wreak all kinds of devastation on European soil or elsewhere. With the finding of these silver disks, with technology that was indescribable and not understood, and with strange creatures in them — which under autopsy were best described as being something like insects, but in some cases with chlorophyll in their systems, while others were not even carbon-based life forms — if I stretch my mind a bit, I can sort of put myself in the shoes of Harry S. Truman, who says, "The world right now is not ready for this, and until we know whether we're dealing with a threat, on top of everything else we're dealing with in the war, we're going to keep this quiet." So, I think most people can understand why the government in the 1940s might have chosen silence.

But as the years moved forward, there was definitely a hostile policy against UFOs in the early 1950s. Leonard String-field, who wrote a very important book called *Situation Red* in 1977,[5] describes death-bed testimonies by military people and scientists who were involved with the retrieval of these crashed disks and bodies. One of the things that Len Stringfield told me is that he himself served in the Air Force, and he remembers that in those early years of the 1950s, there was a standing order in the United States Armed Forces to shoot down unidentified craft in the sky. Well, that story contradicts the rumors that we immediately went into some sort of alliance with whatever this intelligence was that was behind these crashed disks and bodies.

Assuming, as Len said, that we could not beat them — in fact, he said we lost many lives trying to bring down UFOs — the common cliche is that we should try to join them. And this may be when the government decided to precipitate some kind of agreement. So far, I don't know anyone who has a very clear picture on exactly how the communication between the aliens and the government actually started. Did we precipitate something, or did they? I don't know, but I think that most people I've talked with from a variety of sources would agree that at some point in the 1950s to the '60s, our government was in communication with one of these life forms, and that some sort of agreement was struck to exchange their technology for their being able to come and go here with the government's knowledge. I don't know if that's true, but that is a scenario that has been described by many people.

Then, by the 1960s to the '70s, it would appear that our government, if it did in fact have any kind of agreement with these alien life forms, came to the conclusion that whatever was expected from these aliens was not forthcoming, or that they could not be trusted. Since then, the government has been in a mode of, "We still can't tell the public, because we still don't know what we're dealing with, so we'd better keep a lid on this until we know exactly what they want."

Then, in the 1980s, there appeared to be all kinds of efforts to leak a lot of material about these Grays. There was my April, 1983 episode at Kirtland Air Force Base, for example, when an AFOSI agent showed me a briefing paper for the President of the United States about all this [described below]. Later, William Moore and others received the so-called MJ-12 briefing document, which they released in 1987. There were other people in the media who were shown a variety of different pieces of this story in the '80s, as if someone were very interested in media reaction to stories and documents about our government's involvement with extraterrestrials.

Now, as we enter the 1990s, I would say that the tone of what is happening is more serious and more sober. I don't know where it's leading. I know that when I see a newspaper headline, as appeared in May [1990], that Dan Quayle, speaking before the Aeronautics and Astronautics Association in Washington, DC, joins them in a call to use Star Wars nuclear weaponry to blast asteroids headed for the earth,[6] I begin to wonder: Does someone have information about something else out there that none of us know about, and are we getting close to a time when it may be imperative that all of us be told?

RS: Do you think that releasing the full weight of this story to the public could be counterproductive or dangerous? I've heard this idea from a number of psychologists who have just started looking seriously into the UFO phenomenon.

LH: It's a hard question for me to answer, because I've been on this story for ten years, and it's my personal opinion that the world of humans deserves to know at least as much as I know. There is something out of kilter when only a few people have the right to keep something as important as intrusion by an alien life form completely under wraps from the planet that is being intruded upon. That bothers me. At some fundamental human level, we are living a lie on this planet.

Now, whether or not all the information that is contained in the various military and intelligence files, if dumped on the planet in one fell swoop, could be digested and absorbed by the planet easily, I don't know. But somehow we have to come more into sync with the truth. We must come to a point where people are no longer ridiculed because they describe accurately and honestly what they see, when it involves some kind of unidentified object in the sky, animal mutilations, human abductions, all the things that many of us know happen often on this planet and that are associated with a phenomenon and a technology that is not terrestrial. It's been very clear that ridicule has been used as a tool by disinformation campaigns of the intelligence agencies to keep the public at bay, away from the UFO story. Well, it just has to come to an end. That would be a very positive step, I think.

In order for that to happen, I think, it's going to take some formal statement by President Bush and the Joint Chiefs of Staff, and various other leaders, perhaps other countries, to finally say, "Yes, we do have some craft and we do have some bodies, and we have kept this story quiet for several decades through various administrations because we did not know if we were dealing with a national security threat. Now we have decided that we are going to share all this with you, because..." But what follows that "because," I don't know.

RS: Is it possible that the government is purposely allowing and even promoting the slow unravelling of this alien cover-up, and if so, is there any evidence to support this concept?

LH: In 1983, I was shown and told a number of things by a variety of government sources. One of the details I've never forgotten was the statement that *The Day the Earth Stood Still*, the famous 1950s movie classic about an extraterrestrial who comes here with a robot, was one of the first government tests of public reaction to such an event. And, if you'll recall, in that particular science fiction film, the technology that the extraterrestrial had could stop all electrical and elctromagnetic machinery, and that was the big climax of the movie, that nothing could function. Well, the demonstration of that kind of power and technology may have been just the tip of the iceberg. And maybe the government wanted to know if there would be any kind of reaction from the public, even seeing that much in a film. So, if they started with *The Day the Earth Stood Still*, and you come up through various movies and television shows such as *Star Trek*, and you begin to see that many facets of the current UFO phenomenon in all of its large complexity have been discussed in some fashion in so many different television and film stories, perhaps the Central Intelligence Agency and others have been working behind the scenes through their own script writers and people placed in key positions in Los Angeles and New York to make sure they could keep testing aspects of the story on an unwitting public. No one would know that it was not science fiction, and they would have good litmus tests of people's reactions.

RS: One can also look at the science fiction phenomenon as serving the opposite purpose, that you would release movies like this to desensitize the public to the concept, so that when you hear stories of flying saucers you think, my God, it's just some people who have overdosed on *Star Trek*. You could interpret this as actually serving the cover-up as well.

LH: I do think it works both ways. I think that the more media that is out there concerning the extraterrestrial phenomenon, including things like *War of the Worlds* that have even dealt with animal mutilations and using blood to create food, the more some people will then ignore anything that comes up in the real headlines. But other people begin to pay more attention. At least, I've found this to be the case. So, the population may be evolving at different levels in different ways. All of it is probably of great interest to the government, because they're the ones who have to deal with the large social implications.

RS: Some people speculate that the human race is poised for initiation into some sort of galactic federation or some greater, increased awareness of our place in the cosmos. In some quarters, you even hear the idea that some event is going to take place in the near future that will reveal the UFO phenomenon on a grand scale. Do you have any thoughts on those scenarios?

LH: On April 9, 1983, I was taken onto the Kirtland Air Force Base in Albuquerque, into an office where an Air Force Office of Special Investigations agent pulled out an envelope and said his superiors had asked him to show these pages to me. They contained a summary of this government's retrieval of crashed disks and alien bodies, including a live alien from a crash near Roswell in 1949. The paper said that this extraterrestrial had been taken to Los Alamos National Laboratory, where it had been kept until it died of unknown causes on June 18, 1952. Then the paper summarized some of the information that had been learned from this distinctly alien life form about our planet and its civilization's involvement with this planet. One of the paragraphs said, "All questions and mysteries about the evolution of Homo sapiens on this planet have been answered, and this project is closed."

I remember reading those words, and reading them a second time, and reading them a third time as the implications of such a startling sentence washed over me. Because the paper was implying that this gray alien life form had been able to answer all of the government's questions about the evolution of Homo sapiens. Further, it stated in the paper that these gray extraterrestrials had been personally involved in the genetic manipulation of already evolving primates on this planet, suggesting that Cro-Magnon was the result of genetic manipulation by the gray extraterrestrials. Well, if any or all of that is true, then what we could be coming up to, after decades of animal mutilations and human abductions and UFO flaps and all of the drama associated with the phenomenon over the last four or five decades, might be some kind of an introduction between them and us.

RS: How do you know, when you were taken to this Air Force base, that you weren't basically subjected to disinformation, and that you weren't shown false documents in an effort to lead you and other researchers astray, to perpetrate a myth in our society for some other reason?

LH: First of all, by the time I got to Kirtland Air Force Base, the animal mutilation phenomenon had been going strong for over fifteen years, since at least 1967 when I was still in school. The UFO phenomenon had been reported, according to Jacques Vallee, as far back as 40,000 years ago. The human abduction story had been reported publicly since 1963. And all of that was completely and totally independent of the pages that Richard Doty showed me in that office in 1983. The pages that he showed me, interestingly enough, have been reinforced in the last two years by sources having absolutely nothing to do with any of the people in 1983. I feel that if it had all been disinformation, then as time went on it all should have just sort of sifted away like dead sand. In fact, what Richard Doty showed me seems to get stronger in terms of supporting material.

RS: Doty himself is accused of being a disinformer. Some people claim that he led Paul Bennewitz and Bill Moore astray with all kinds of false information, culminating in the infamous affair where Bill Moore was actually playing the role of a disinformer on Mr. Bennewitz. How far can you trust Doty?

LH: I don't understand him or what his actual task was. During the two or three months when he talked to me quite a bit, he said I was to go back East to screen several thousand feet of film that had been taken in the 1940s to the 1960s, of crashed disks and bodies and a landing at Holloman Air Force Base. He spent a great deal of time discussing arrangements that would have to be made for me to screen and handle the film. He spoke as if he were simply following the orders of some superior and always said he could do nothing on his own. He never expressed to me any sense of his own self-importance.

I don't know what the truth was about his relationship to, let's say, an MJ-12 group. It certainly seemed as if the context within which he was operating during that period of time was leading up to my being shown some film. That didn't happen, but why? I don't know. Was he actually doing what he did because they had decided to show me some film that might be used in the Home Box Office special that I was working on at the time? That's as likely a scenario as that they decided to show me several pieces of paper simply to get my reaction. But if they thought that I would run out into the streets with this astonishing material, they guessed wrong, because to me it was the kind of information that you keep quiet until you have more supporting evidence.

And that's one of the ironies in all this, that material such as Doty showed me has such astonishing implications that you tend *not* to talk about it. I and others who get into this story find ourselves suppressing conversations and information. And that may have been exactly the same position that the government took. That's one of the odd loops in this big story.

RS: Do you yourself have information at your disposal that you would continue to keep secret and not disclose?

LH: Yes.

RS: And why is that?

LH: [Editor's note: At Linda's insistence, her answer to this question was not recorded. She subsequently told me that the nature of certain information known to her was such that "I don't want to be the one who discusses these things at the present time." She declined to elaborate further.]

RS: If you were to play devil's advocate against your own position regarding the alien presence, can you conceive of any credible explanation for the evidence you have amassed that relies only on earth-based phenomena? For example, John Judge, a researcher on government conspiracy issues, claims that much of the so-called "alien" technology that people observe as UFOs was created by the Nazis shortly before the end of World War II, was then taken over and elaborated by both the Soviet Union and the United States, and that now what we're seeing is really super-secret, super-sophisticated terrestrial technology.[7] Is there any evidence that can support that, in your view?

LH: You should talk with Robert Lazar about that. I don't believe Lazar was dealing with anything terrestrial. You need to hear the first-hand testimony of a guy who had his mind completely stretched by what he was asked to work on at S 4. [See next chapter.] I believe the man is telling the truth when he says that he was working on an antimatter propulsion system involving gravity wave amplifiers with no connecting or moving parts. He says it's preposterous to assert that any of this was terrestrial, when we don't even understand what gravity is yet.

I have confidential sources — they'll never see the light of day because they have to protect themselves — but they have talked to me in enormous detail about craft and about the bodies that have been autopsied. I don't have any doubt that these people are telling the truth. And that doesn't have anything to do with Nazi Germany's efforts to create some sort of round flying machine. We're talking about something quite separate and different.

I want to lift this to a little higher ground. I think that in the last year, one of the most provocative angles on this whole UFO phenomenon was described to me by a man who, for lack of a better definition, I will simply say has a profession connected with aerospace and aircraft. He came to see me. He had read my book, *An Alien Harvest,* and he said he felt that I was on the track of a lot of things that he knew to be correct. Then he said, "When people describe seeing moving, unidentified lights in the sky, consider the possibility that these are moving windows, moving electromagnetic portals between universes."

When he said that, it suddenly occurred to me that the phenomenon could be both hard — the craft at S4 that scientists could work on — and yet also something even beyond the imaginings of most people, like electromagnetic openings between time and space here and time and space somewhere else. And ever since, it has made this whole universe around me that much more complex and bizarre. It has made me think a great deal about the fact that we are dealing with a phenomenon, as my friend Jacques Vallee has said many times, that doesn't fit easily into the category of simply being extraterrestrial [see Briefing]. So much of it has other-dimensional qualities. We have this big, complex story with everything from animal mutilations and human abductions to the craft and the retrieved bodies, but there is also this very large and not well-understood complexity of the phenomenon having an effect on space and time. That, I think, is how you explain missing time cases. We're dealing with a technology that literally has the ability to warp space and time.

When you get to that level in this story, I think that is where we're eventually going to hear some of the most exciting information, both from scientists and perhaps from the aliens themselves. What we are beginning to approach is a whole new higher ground, a completely different understanding of ourselves and this universe. Space, time, gravity and electromagnetic fields are going to take on a new reality, and moving backwards and forwards in time may actually become a reality.

BRIEFING:

Beyond the Extraterrestrial Hypothesis

The extraterrestrial hypothesis, or ETH, proposes that genuine UFOs and their intelligent occupants originate from another planet in a star system probably similar to our own. Since the time of the Roswell incident, most serious UFO researchers have subscribed to the ETH, but in recent years there has been a growing counter-argument based on the observation that the ETH does not adequately explain all the known data. Within the ranks of ufology, the most eloquent case against the ETH has been put forth by Dr. Jacques Vallee.

Vallee is an astrophysicist, computer scientist and UFO researcher who states that UFOs and "aliens" are physically real and that they interact frequently with humans — often with traumatic results — yet are probably not of extraterrestrial origin. In his bestselling book, Dimensions: A *Casebook of Alien Contact* (Contemporary Books, 1988), Vallee poses several arguments against the ETH.

First, he says, there are simply too many encounters. Vallee has collected his data by going to the physical locations of sightings and landings all over the world. He has taken first-hand testimony from hundreds of witnesses. With the skeptical precision of a trained scientist, he has weighed his data and found many of the eyewitness accounts to be reliable — so reliable, in fact, that they leave the impression of an *absurd* number of encounters, if the UFOs must travel many light-years to reach the earth.

Second, the apparent physics of UFO behavior makes no sense in our time-space. The often-reported propensity of UFOs to change shape or disappear instantly suggests that they might appear as holographic projections at times, or even slip between our own time-space and some parallel dimension at will. Such possibilities neither require nor even favor the notion of extraterrestrial origin.

Third, the profusion of reported types of "aliens," as well as reported alien behavior, again strikes Vallee as absurd. However, this does not mean he discounts the reports. Taking them as serious efforts to describe real experience, Vallee says the so-called aliens don't fit any logical pattern of extraterrestrial visitors. Tracing back through the long history of reported humanoid "super-beings" in religious and folkloric literature, he suggests that today's "aliens" might be a modern analog to ancient gods, demons and faeries. The parallels are particularly striking in regard to claims of abduction. From ancient times to the present day, he argues, all these beings might be part of a "control system" somehow linked to the evolution of human consciousness, culture and technical knowledge. Again, the extraterrestrial explanation is neither necessary nor adequate.

In sum, says Vallee, "the extraterrestrial theory is not good enough, because it is not strange enough to explain the facts."

Once a firm proponent of the ETH, Vallee found himself increasingly at odds with other researchers once he started arguing against what he terms a "first-level interpretation" of the ETH. He agrees that it remains one of the hypotheses to be considered, but he advocates a "second-level" interpretation that takes into account the ability of UFOs to manipulate the physical and psychic environment of witnesses. Today, his ideas are gaining acceptance as part of an emerging theoretical synthesis that includes the extraterrestrial possibility alongside many others. In this new framework, "alien" is seen as a general — and no doubt inadequate — term for a huge diversity of intelligent life and super-technology now impinging on human awareness. In this light, "aliens" could originate from distant stars, nearby planets, parallel dimensions, the inner earth or the human psyche with equal likelihood. The final answer might be "all of the above," but it's much too soon to tell. — ML

Chapter Three
Bob Lazar: Alien Technology in Government Hands

Bob Lazar caused a sensation in 1989 with the claim that he had been involved in a super-secret government project to study the propulsion system of an alien spacecraft held by the military at a facility called S 4 near Groom Lake, Nevada. He first appeared as a black silhouette labeled "Dennis" on a Las Vegas television news program in the spring of 1989, then came forward undisguised as the star attraction in a nine-part special report, "UFOs: The Best Evidence," anchored by Las Vegas newsman George Knapp for CBS affiliate KLAS-TV Channel 8 in October of that year. The special report detailed not only Lazar's unusual claims but also his troubling personal saga during and after his alleged employment at S 4.

If Lazar is telling the truth, his story has devastating implications. Needless to say, numerous investigators have poked into his background, only to find that Lazar's education and employment records don't always match his claims. George Knapp went further than most in trying to track down Lazar's real history and found himself in agreement with Lazar that the young scientist's records seem to have been intentionally altered. Knapp stated on the air that he thought Lazar was telling the truth. Later, in *UFO* magazine,[1] Knapp emphasized that Lazar's story has stayed consistent from the beginning, that he had worked for Los Alamos National Laboratory as claimed, and that a recently-acquired W-2 form showed he had also worked for the Office of Naval Intelligence, his alleged employer on the alien project. In any case, the "real Bob Lazar" remains a topic of hot debate.

Ralph Steiner [RS] and I arranged for a face-to-face interview with Bob [BL] on September 22, 1990. Joining us was a nuclear physicist [PH] currently employed at a major research

Bob Lazar

facility, whose name is withheld on request. Also present was Las Vegas businessman Gene Huff [GH], who probably knows more of the Lazar story than anyone but Lazar himself, and who has defended Bob's veracity from the beginning. The resulting conversation, which comprises this chapter, is the most complete telling of Lazar's story published to date. By prior agreement, the conversation excludes certain technological details of the alien craft that Bob claims to have studied.

However, some of those details may be forthcoming soon. "The Lazar Tape, and Excerpts from the Government Bible" is Bob's own video presentation of his story, due out in the summer of 1991. In Bob's words, "Being ignorant of the established science regarding disks and interstellar travel causes one to spend countless hours trying to reason through the unsubstantiated conjecture perpetuated by charlatans....Much of what is considered magic in ufology is unexplained science, and 'The

Lazar Tape' is the explanation in layman's terms." For more information, write to: The Lazar Tape, 1324 S. Eastern, Las Vegas, NV 89104. — ML

Michael Lindemann: There's a lot of rumor and theory floating around about you, Bob, and during this conversation I hope we can sort out some of the truth from the nonsense. To start with, why did you go to S 4, and why did you leave?

Bob Lazar: A lot of that information hasn't been brought out at all, and at first it would have been a little painful to bring out. I had no idea what the job was really going to be. As far as I knew, I was going to be working on an advanced propulsion system. As the interviews continued and things progressed, I came to believe it was going to be a field propulsion system, and I was elated. This was fantastic. And that was it.

As for going out to S 4, I originally didn't even know there was an S 4. I thought I was going to be at Area 51, where an awful lot of projects are done, including a lot of the black projects such as the SR-71 and so forth. In fact, I know several people who worked at Area 51, so I didn't think it was going to be any extremely secret project, anything along the lines of alien technology. In fact, the way I learned there was an S 4 was the first time I got out there. We landed at Area 51, and moments later we got on a bus and started driving and driving. And I realized, gee, I don't work at Area 51. Then, about fifteen miles south of there, I was told that S 4 was the designation. In any case, I went out there because I thought I'd be involved in an interesting project.

ML: Who told you that? And who solicited your services?

BL: No one solicited my services. I sent resumes out to a few labs. I really wanted to get back into mainstream science. I also sent a resume to Ed Teller, whom I'd met at Los Alamos in June of 1982. We'd had a talk. We kind of became, not really friends, but acquaintances. In fact, on the day I met him, a newspaper from Los Alamos had an article and photo of the jet car I built on the front page. That's how I met him. I was going to his lecture, and I got there probably 20 or 30 minutes early. As I walked up to the lecture hall, he was at the side of the building, outside the lecture hall. There's a coin-operated newspaper machine there, and Ed was leaning on the wall reading the paper on the front page. So I felt, hey, I'd like to meet him, and I said, "By the way, that's me you're reading about," so on and so forth. He had a couple of minutes, and there's a little coffeeshop near there, so we sat down and talked for a bit.

In any case, I made reference to our meeting when I wrote him. I said I had left Los Alamos, and the things I'd worked on — the polarized proton targets and so forth — and he remembered me. Some time later, I received a call from him. How this progressed, I don't exactly remember. I think he said, you'll be receiving a call from... or, I forwarded your resume to... someone down at EG&G. But I'd say it was no more than ten or fifteen minutes after he hung up that I got a call to come down for an interview at EG&G Special Projects. So that's how my services were solicited, if you can even call it that.

GH: That's when Teller told you that he wouldn't actively be hiring you, that he was the chief consultant, but he would have the other guy call you.

BL: Right.

ML: Did EG&G eventually hire you?

BL: No.

ML: Did the Office of Naval Intelligence hire you?

BL: Right. EG&G has nothing to do with it. There are several other departments that used that EG&G building and their air transportation out there, because they have a lot of projects going on at Area 51, and it's their fleet of planes. All they really used the EG&G building for was the interview. So, some people say it's a front, and I think I've said it before; but I don't know if it's used as a front. They're just using their facilities.

Now, as to why I left, that's kind of a bizarre and complicated story. After I had gone out there — actually, even before — I signed consents to have my telephone conversations monitored, spontaneous searches of my car and house and so forth, which occurred all the time. In fact, I have a friend who worked up at the Tonopah test range on the stealth fighter, and we would talk on the phone occasionally. And whoever they were — I don't know what department they came from — they would appear at the house moments after a phone call. They'd have a transcript of my phone conversation with things circled in red, and they'd want me to explain what we were talking about or referring to. This led me to believe that they were close, they immediately made transcripts of whatever I was saying, and they analyzed the transcripts and got to me instantaneously. Certainly, they were really on the ball as far as that was concerned. In any case, the phone conversations were definitely being monitored, and there was a very close watch on what was going on. Also on my personal life.

At the time, my wife and I were having some difficulties, essentially beginning to drift apart. I don't think I've mentioned this publicly, although George Knapp and others knew it on the side. At the time, she was having an affair with someone, and of course everything was going on over the phone. They'd converse, and everyone knew about it except me. The FBI, or whoever was the investigating agency, was wondering what was going on. And this was at the time I was being called up to S 4. I wasn't formally hired to come out there every day. I never started a regular work schedule. I was going out sporadically. They were really juggling around the idea, should he stay, is there going to be too much of a traumatic strain in his life when he finds out what's going on, is he going to be a security risk, and so forth.

As it turned out, that's why my clearance was denied.

They knew something was going to come to a head and then I was going to be, in their words, "emotionally unstable" for some time afterwards, just after being brought into this project. They didn't want any loose screws around.

RS: Was this before or after you took Gene and John [Lear] out to the test site?[2]

BL: After.

GH: Everyone thought that he got kicked out of the program and lost his security clearance because he took us out there, but in fact that was not true. He was still in the program. But then there was a dry spell when they didn't call him for a long time, and it was driving him crazy. As it ended up, they were hearing his now ex-wife on the phone with her boyfriend. They didn't want to break the news to him that she was having an affair. Then one day, after she told Bob, she called her mother and said, "I had an affair, and I told Bob." Once they heard that she told Bob, they called him down and rejected his security clearance, saying that you have to be emotionally, financially and every kind of stable to get that high a security clearance. Didn't they even say you could re-apply in six to nine months?

BL: Right. That's why I left S 4. I didn't actually leave, they denied my clearance. But that also left them in somewhat of a predicament, because here they had basically told me three-quarters of the story of what's going on, I had hands-on experience with everything, and that's when tensions began to rise, as soon as I got out. But that's the hiring and firing portion of the story.

ML: Are you saying that you took Gene and John Lear out to watch the little blinking light over the mountains...

BL: Gene, John Lear, Jim Taliani, my ex-wife, her sister...that was it.

GH: Not all at the same time. Those were several different trips.

ML:....you took those people out there, and that in itself did not constitute enough of a breach of your security vows?

BL: (laughing) Oh yes, to them it did. But they never said, "We're pulling your security clearance, you're no longer working, never come back," or whatever. I was just debriefed the next day, which was quite an unpleasant experience. Essentially, they gave me a slap on the wrist.

ML: Taking Gene and some others out to watch a little light over the mountains is, let's say, one level of indiscretion. Going on television is quite another. What led you to that step?

BL: That's a good question. What led me to that step?...[to GH] When did I get shot? Was that after or before?

GH: Well, at first he did the basic story with George Knapp, just for safe-keeping. Up to a month before George Knapp's television special, he had not even given George permission to use anything about him.

BL: I'm thinking about all the way back to when I went on silhouette as "Dennis."

GH: You got shot at after that.

BL: After? I thought that was the motivation for doing that. Maybe I was crazy! (laughs) George had called me when we were at John Lear's house, and I said, "No, no, no! Forget it!" He kept on me, and I think I finally agreed to, in silhouette. We had originally talked about digitizing the face and the voice, and I guess in the back of my mind I thought they wouldn't recognize me, or something like that. It's a while ago. So much has gone on, it's hard to get everything in chronological order. But why specifically I did that, I don't know. Maybe I felt obligated to do it. That wasn't the brightest thing I've ever done, because it caused a lot of problems immediately afterwards.

ML: You expressed a lot of frustration in the public statements that you made, about the poor quality of research that was going on around you, the idea that maybe this was the story of the century, and it was bottled up and being handled by second-rate people and so forth. At least the constraints on it were such that the science had to be second-rate.

BL: Yes, it was a two-fold thing. First, we're talking about the story in general, which is of great historical value, and second, the way the science was being handled. Those were my two main complaints.

ML: And how about the way you were treated?

BL: Well, of course, I wasn't thrilled with the way I was treated, or the way anyone else was being treated, but I could almost accept that in view of what was going on. That wasn't a major complaint.

ML: Are you saying that, given the circumstances, even though it wasn't very pleasant, you regarded the treatment as logical?

BL: Not logical. Acceptable.

ML: I'd like to speculate for a moment. There's been a lot of talk recently that the overall cover-up is shifting into a new phase — that it had been conducted along fairly stable parameters for a very long time, but that within the last several years it has shifted — and that what you did, whether you intended it or not, essentially played into the changed nature of the cover-up, which is now, let's say, to orchestrate the gradual revelation of the whole story. What's your sense about all that?

BL: That is certainly possible. I won't deny that it's possible, although if it was done, it certainly was not done with my knowledge. That's kind of the "controlled release of information" theory.

GH: It could have happened, yes, but is that what you think happened? That's another question.

BL: No, I don't think that's what happened. The reason being, how would they know I was going to release any information? That was certainly not my intention at the beginning. Gene being my close friend, I didn't say a word to him. I didn't say a word to my wife. Everything was on the QT. And I really did keep within the constraints of the program as far as the Secrecy Act. I can't see how they would have guessed.

ML: There's the theory that they planned you to release it, which I don't particularly buy either. But there's another scenario where they say, "Oh look, Lazar is going to release this, what a great opportunity." That is, you made your decisions for reasons entirely your own, and that actually served their purposes.

BL: It's possible.

ML: Do you see any evidence that it's been played that way?

BL: No.

GH: You're giving too little credit, actually, to the way he released it. He waited, even with George Knapp, and then suddenly it was on television. Now, they can say after the fact, "Oh, we planned Lazar to do that." But once he went on the record, what could they do? Arrest him? Kill him? And prove that everything he's saying is true? So, not to give him a pat on the back, but the way it happened, they were probably out-smarted just a little bit. They really didn't know how many people he had talked to and to what extent he had told them what was going on. We knew they were monitoring the phone. They didn't know whether what he and I and everyone else said on the phone was true or not. They'd have had to shut up a lot of people, as far as they knew. So actually, he forced their hand more than the general public probably thinks.

PH: So you think that it had been secretive enough that it wouldn't have been detected? Well, how about when you were in silhouette? I think they figured out who you were, right?

BL: Instantly. Right after I left there, [security officer] Dennis Mariani called...

PH: Then they could have taken you and shut you up.

BL: Immediately thereafter, I was shot at. But again, that was the worst shot in the history of mankind...

PH: I think the implication is, for some reason, they're going to let some of what you're saying go out.

GH: A couple of days before the TV special, the Air Force Office of Special Investigations [AFOSI] detained a friend of his...

BL: They went and pulled him out of work...

GH: ...and wanted to find out where Bob was, because they "wanted to give him some help." But this might be a case of the AFOSI not being in deep enough to actually know what's going on. Because the people at S 4 obviously knew where he lived. They'd been to his house a million times. What do you mean, where is he?

BL: But at that time, I was house-sitting at another house.

GH: That's true. But the AFOSI was trying to get hold of him before the special aired and couldn't find him. And then the special hit.

PH: I guess I wouldn't put it past them to be totally inept, either.

BL: Certainly, luck played a portion in it.

PH: I wouldn't be talking with you if I thought that you were going to tell me something that was really a matter of national security. They've had plenty of time to tell you no, plenty of time to stop you, and they didn't. So presumably, most of what you're saying is acceptable to them, and it probably isn't considered a matter of national security, or you couldn't be saying it.

GH: But what can they do now? They can kill him, but if they do, what does that say?

PH: I don't think they'd do that. For instance, when the nuclear weapons program was beginning at Los Alamos, there were people who went to some of the bars and started bragging a little too much. And they stopped them. Those people disappeared. I don't know if they ever resurfaced. I don't think they killed them, because they don't tend to do things like that, but I'm sure they locked them up, because they disappeared. Or else they told them persuasively enough, "Go away, and if we catch you talking about it again, you're going to be the most unhappy person on the face of the earth." They get people to stop. I'm sure they could persuade you to stop too, if they went at it aggressively enough.

BL: But they did. They threatened me, with someone's face two or three inches from mine. They went over and over how "We will kill you," and...

PH: It's interesting that you went ahead...

GH: Also, consider the frame of mind he was in about his wife, after what he found out. There was literally a point in time when it gave him enough intestinal fortitude that he didn't care if he lived or died.

BL: Right. In fact, that was one of the key things. What they were telling me was really secondary. There was one time when a guy was threatening me, during debriefing or whatever — he was really jumping on me. "We're talking bodily injury, death, a mental institution." And as he went over and over it, it almost became like I was in shell-shock. I was sitting there listening to him, and I cracked a smile. And they couldn't believe it. I just started smiling. I don't know why. And then they said, "Oh yeah? Well then, we'll get your wife." It seemed like at that moment, they really had nothing else to say.

GH: "OK, go get her."

BL: Right.

GH: It was obviously a rare occasion, and I guess we'll never actually know what their thought was. We do feel, though, that there was somebody, probably Dennis Mariani, who got in big trouble. His job is to stay on these people. They go to great lengths to use intimidation, anything to keep people quiet. Not only did Bob not stay quiet, he did a television special. Now, who do you think had to pay the price for that? Someone did.

ML: When you were a guest on the Billy Goodman radio show in November of 1989,[3] a man referring to himself as a "Mercury worker" called in to say that some other people were going to come forward. Has anything happened?

BL: Those guys are a bunch of clowns. I really don't know what they're about. We got a call later that month from someone at the Billy Goodman show, saying this guy had just contacted him and said all these Mercury workers are being held at S 4, they're being tortured, and can we help. You know, I think he's just a nut-case.

GH: We asked him questions, like have their families been notified? Does anybody know they're missing? Nobody could answer these questions.

BL: What do they expect me to do? Run down to S 4 and break them out? It's ridiculous.

RS: There's another factor that makes me think you might have been set up to disseminate information. You've mentioned that along with hardware information, in the document room you saw autopsy reports and other information on the extraterrestrials. Why would that be in there, in that compartmentalized situation?

BL: That's a question I've never been able to answer. But again I'll say, there was not complete information on everything. It was like a small briefing, maybe a page and a half, on many things that were going on. Now, there are many theories I've heard about it, and some I have myself. Maybe it's just to relieve the initial curiosity. "This is basically what's going on, now shut up and don't ask any more questions," as opposed to "Just work on the flying saucer and don't ask any questions at all."

RS: Did they have photos in there?

BL: Yes.

ML: Photos of extraterrestrials?

BL: Yes. They were more or less autopsy reports. They were bust shots, essentially, with the chest cavity open, and some of the organs on the side. Most of the photographs were of organs, or *the* organ, I should say. What did that have to do with me? I have no medical background. I'm very weak in biology. And I find it difficult to believe it was put in there by accident. There was obviously some reason for it, but what that is, I don't know.

GH: We've got to get this straight. The fact is, when he was in the room with the 120-odd briefings, there was an overview of numerous things: autopsies, the alien civilization, all kinds of things. And it looks like this was probably a place that they would take any scientist to give a briefing on what's going on. What he read in the overview of the propulsion systems in these briefings was further elaborated and substantiated in depth, being his particular field. So it looks like this room and these briefings would have been a place that you would also bring a biologist, or a chemist, or someone who's going to be working on alien cadavers, and they too get an overview of propulsion, and all the chemistry and biology and everything, because you can't take scientists and say, "Go do this," and not expect them to ask, "By the way, are these aliens?" You have to let them know what's going on. So it's strictly conjecture, but it looks like it would be to brief scientists on the overview, and then they were given elaborate supporting information in their own individual fields.

BL: One of the main questions that I have is: Why pick me for that project?

ML: Do you have an answer to that?

BL: No, I don't. Certainly, I'm not the foremost physicist working on that type of propulsion. I have no idea of metallurgy. So many things are required in that project that I have very little knowledge of. I really worked in a fairly narrow field when it came to that particular branch of physics, though I have a very wide range of interests and am more or less of a maverick, so to speak. I usually go about things in a strange way. I don't follow a standard, set procedure. I usually walk off the beaten path and try something completely bizarre. I had great success with that at Los Alamos and in many other things I've done. This is my own theory. Perhaps they wanted someone from left field to come and just do something strange, try to approach it from a different angle. If that's what they were looking for, fine, then they did find it. Maybe I might choose someone like myself to do that. But as far as a top-notch nuclear physicist, no, I don't fit in that category, though that's what belonged there. And I didn't see, not only any equipment like that, I didn't see any people that fit that category.

RS: Would you basically say the research situation was crimped, with a paucity of equipment and personnel to do the job?

BL: Certainly there were not enough personnel to accomplish anything. In fact, how they even got that far is beyond me, with 22 people. Now, there is a possibility that there were more that I didn't see, but from what I understood and what I read in the paperwork, that's what composed the project. As far as equipment, no, there's not nearly enough equipment there. We're talking just minimal.

PH: How much trouble do they have operating, say, the sport model? [see Briefing, next page] Can they make it perform its whole envelope? Do they have trouble and crash them once in a while?

BL: I really don't know. None of the disks looked damaged to me, and I would expect to find one dented up, if that's how they learned to fly, but I didn't see that. As far as how proficient they are in the operation of the craft, the navigation, I have no idea. I only saw the sport model operate at close range once. It didn't seem out of control at any time.

PH: Do you think there was somebody in it, running it?

BL: Yes, I do, though I can't confirm that. I can only assume there were some men inside who were operating the craft.

PH: Did it maneuver much?

BL: It just shifted to the left, shifted to the right. It didn't do any radical maneuvers while I was there. In fact, that Wednesday night when we were caught was supposed to be a high-performance test of the sport model. It would have been fantastic video, if we had not gotten caught that night.

GH: And they cancelled it because we stayed out there in the desert so long.

PH: How close were you to the thing when it actually lifted off?

BL: I'm a poor judge of distances, but I would imagine fifty feet, maybe a hundred feet. I was standing just inside the hangar door, and it was just outside.

ML: Do you know the circumstances by which we acquired the sport model?

BL: No.

ML: Did you have any sense during the time you were there that this research was being conducted with any kind of cooperative agreement with aliens?

BL: (long pause, nervous laugh): There's a possibility of it, if one document I read was true. Now, I have no

BRIEFING:

Lazar's Terminology

Bob Lazar burst upon the scene in mid-1989 with a story that introduced several new words to the vocabulary of UFO research and lore. For readers not familiar with Lazar's terminology, a brief glossary follows.

Element 115: a super-heavy substance that supposedly powers the reactor in alien craft. "115" refers to the theoretical atomic number of this element, placing it well beyond any element known on earth. Lazar claims that this element is not radioactive, and according to theoretical physics this is possible. Other properties of 115 are described later in this chapter.

Gravity amplifiers: a set of three devices, located on the underside of an alien craft, which amplify and focus a gravity wave (q.v.) produced by a reactor (q.v.). The action of the gravity amplifiers enables the craft to travel inter-stellar distance in a short period of time by "bending" or "folding" space.

Gravity wave: a wave that propagates spontaneously

from the nucleus of super-heavy elements. In an alien craft, Lazar claims, this wave is produced in the reactor and is directed upward through a central tube called a **wave guide**, then downward along the sides of the craft to the gravity amplifiers. Control of gravity waves is the heart of alien propulsion technology.

Reactor: Superficially similar to reactors built on earth, the alien variety is a hemispherical power source no bigger than half a basketball, located in the center of the craft described by Lazar. The reactor produces gravity waves from element 115, and megawatts of electricity from a matter-antimatter reaction.

Sport model: Lazar's name for the craft he claims to have worked on at S-4. This was one of nine different craft he saw at the facility, but the only one he describes in detail and the only one he saw in operation. He has likened its appearance to a craft alleg-edly photographed in Switzerland by Billy Meier. Meier's photos are printed in *UFO...Contact from the Pleiades, Vol I,* by Lee Elders, Wendelle Stevens et al (revised edition 1980, Genesis III Publishing, Phoenix, AZ). — ML

reason to suspect it was disinforma-tion or untrue anyway, but there was reference in it to an incident. At one time, there was apparently some exchange of information between living aliens and either scientists or engineers, whoever was working on the craft; and there was apparently a conflict at the time. That, I believe, was in 1978 or '79. In either case, the document did go into a brief explanation. I don't know if it was really even an information exchange, but the document claimed that there were living aliens working on something there, and I can only assume that there was an interaction.

If that is true, that brings to light the possibility that maybe the craft was given to us. Maybe it was not a crash retrieval. But it also brings up other questions: How come they haven't returned? Why isn't this continuing today? Why is the S 4 project there to begin with? Why should we have to back-engineer something if we were given it? They didn't give us the instruction book on how to operate the craft, the technical specifications or whatever.

ML: I wonder if you'd say more specifically what you read in that report.

BL: Apparently there were alien beings working in an isolated lab somewhere. This area was heavily guarded. There was certainly a surplus of military personnel who had side-arms. That's how it was when I was there too, at S 4, where everyone walked around with automatic weapons. From what I understand and can remember, a conflict arose there. One of the military personnel attempted to enter that work area and was motioned to stop. [ML: By an alien?] By an alien, yes. This is how the report was written. An indication was made, referencing the weapon, not to enter the area. I think it was speculation after this point whether there was some sort of field being produced, or something like that, where bringing live ammunition in there might detonate. But it was motioned to leave that there or stop. And instead of doing that, the really brilliant guard or military person took that as kind of a power contest, and he decided to keep progressing. At this point it got really strange, because before he entered the room, he was killed. It really didn't go on with any specifics, except that he died of a head-wound. As soon as that happened, I think, the conflict escalated quite rapidly. The outcome of it was that none of the aliens were killed and all the military personnel were. They all died almost instantly. The report mentioned all head-wounds.

I don't think there was any hostile intent on the alien part. I think it just may have been that they were actually protecting what could have happened. Of course, it could have just been a complete hostile situation where, zap, everyone dies. Now, it didn't mention what weapon was used, in specific how the deaths occurred, but certainly none of the beings themselves were hurt.

PH: Did you read this, or did you hear about it?

BL: This I read.

ML: Was this part of the briefing material at S 4 that you were supposed to read?

BL: This was in a stack of documents that I thumbed through.

Now, I've heard this story repeated, saying this happened in Dulce, New Mexico. Apparently this is where that rumor came from, if this is true.

ML: Where did this event occur, to your knowledge?

BL: This occurred at the Nevada test site, in the Area 51/S 4 area. I don't know specifically where.

ML: And as far as you know, since that time, have there been no aliens on that base?

BL: No, if there even were at that time. But if you're taking that as fact, that is the only mention anywhere of any interaction between us. And that's why I think, again taking that as fact, that we received those craft more by friendly means than by crash-retrieval or stealing them or however else.

RS: What was your task during the ten times or less that you were out there? What specific kinds of tasks were you asked to perform on the drive system?

BL: I hadn't gotten into a solid work schedule. Most of the time I spent there was on demonstrations and just getting caught up on what others had done before me. But certainly my task would have related directly to propulsion. Not even working on the reactor. It was going to narrow down essentially to the gravity amplifiers. They really wanted to know about the two modes of flight. They wanted to know more about the second mode of flight, the long-range traveling in space, and that relied heavily on how the gravity amplifiers worked, the amount of power they put out and of course the physics relating to how the gravity waves propagate, how the reactor powers the gravity amplifiers and how the basic gravity wave is tapped, amplified and phase-shifted.

ML: You were going to be working on the second mode of

flight, but you didn't really get around to it, is that correct?

BL: Well, when I started working on the specific problem, I back-tracked to the reactor. I said, we can't jump right in the middle of it and say, how does this work? We don't even know how it's powered. I started back at the reactor and asked, where is the gravity wave coming from that can even possibly be amplified? Of course, others that had been there before me had narrowed that down to the reactor, but they weren't sure why the gravity wave propagates upward in a wave guide. I had someone bring up that question, and I had never thought about that, even while I was working there. I just assumed it went up, and I really don't know. I assume the wave guide was tuned to it, but we really never did get that deep into it. So, as I began to work there, I began to concentrate on the fuel itself, on the 115, and really just had an overview of the basic propulsion system, how things operated, but never began to narrow down into a specific area. Keep in mind that when I first went out there, they had no idea what the fuel was.

ML: They had not yet identified 115?

BL: I was the one who identified 115. That was my only contribution to the project. And I don't stand on the fact that it's 115, but if it's not, it's 114. It's right in there.

ML: That brings us to a question we discussed before meeting you today. We weren't sure whether 115 was a very precise nomenclature.

BL: No, it's not. I call it 115 because I've gotten used to saying that, but it's certainly right in there.

PH: How did you determine that? Did you put it in a mass spectrograph? How do you figure out what element it was?

BL: Well, there are many different ways, but certainly, a mass spectrograph was one way. We also did all kinds of bizarre things. Los Alamos apparently was involved in some of the analysis of the 115, and I don't know if they knew what they were doing. They were also involved in some of the machining of the 115 pieces.

PH: How stable is the stuff that you had? Is it radioactive, and if so, what is the half-life?

BL: 115 is not radioactive.

PH: Element 115 would be homologous to bismuth, I think, so would it sort of look like lead? Kind of a silvery metal, soft...?

BL: No, it's more of a burnt orange color. And it is extremely soft. You can certainly make an indentation with your fingernail into it. It's heavy. By lifting a small piece of it, you can tell it's not lead. It's amazingly heavy.

ML: So your contribution was identifying this stuff?

BL: Yes, and there again, this confirms what I said, that this project was apparently being worked on for some time, several years I would imagine, and they had no idea what the fuel was. We're talking about a very basic thing, certainly a reasonable starting point.

PH: You had a bunch of Ph.Ds there, right?

BL: I don't know.

GH: [to questioners] Do you know why they needed another man? Did you ever hear that story?

RS: Why don't you go ahead and tell us.

GH: This will show you how elementary the investigation was.

BL: Apparently, they had an operating reactor. I know there were several removed from the crafts, and they were all essentially the same. While a reactor was operating, they wanted to look inside it; and they decided the best way to do that would be to cut it open. Well, the reactor exploded and killed the people that did it. That is certainly not following the scientific method. That's insane. And there again, I was told flat out that I was the direct replacement for the people who were lost in this project. Everything I saw, every step of the way, just showed me that such an incredible project is being handled not only in an unprofessional manner, but it bordered on the ridiculous.

PH: When you say you don't know who was working on it, is it because you were only there for a short time, or they kept it secret, or you don't want to talk about it? If I were going in and there were ten people working on a power system or reactor, and they were trying to figure out what the power source is, I think I'd get a feel for what caliber these guys were, like were they Ph.D. level or were they more engineering oriented or whatever. But they sound like idiots. They sound like military engineers who don't have any sophisticated training.

BL: That's the way it sounded to me, and they could all be military personnel. I may have been the only civilian there. I don't know.

PH: But why don't you know? Because you just weren't there long enough? You must have talked to them, didn't you?

BL: No, that's not how things work. You cannot just start a conversation with someone. They work on the buddy system. You're assigned with one other person, and he is the only person you carry on conversations with, period. As for grabbing someone in the hall, that's out of the question. In fact, even when you go to the bathroom, you're followed by security.

PH: How do you find out what they think they know and what

they've done so far? With briefing documents? You don't talk to people?

BL: Well, I spoke to Barry. He was the guy who was assigned as my partner. Now, I don't know if it would stay this way throughout the whole project. Maybe it was part of the learning experience, or their initiation, whatever it is. But Barry was the one. There was a looseleaf folder, a basic log of the steps that were taken in the analysis...

PH: How long had they been working on the thing?

BL: It seemed like at least a couple of years.

GH: This goes back to your original question, how he got into the program. We thought about that and got the feeling that Teller, for whatever reason, had remembered him and liked him. Bob sent a resume with some patents that he had, things like that, and we got the feeling that possibly he got juiced into the program by Edward Teller. Maybe some people really didn't want him there, which is why he could have been on call to begin with, and why they'd go two weeks and then call and tell him to come out, as though they were just patronizing him to please Edward Teller. [to BL] You know you weren't one of the boys, that's for sure.

BL: Yes, there's no doubt about that.

RS: Well, who are the boys? Is there a litmus test for the people inducted into this program, and what does that consist of? What did you go through?

BL: I went through what seemed to be a standard interview for any job of that sort. In fact, the interview was even less in depth than the one I went through at Los Alamos. There was nothing unusual about it. Now, the security was certainly unusual. I've never had people come and search the house before, I've never had my phone monitored before. But as far as being some sort of test, it seemed like that was determined before anything ever began, without my knowledge. So I really don't know how they decide who's going to get to play, and who's not.

RS: Do you think there's a fundamental tension between the need of this program to find top-notch people to advance the research, and the requirement that it be kept so compartmentalized and so secret?

BL: Yes, I do. But I don't know, and I'm certainly not convinced, that they're looking for top-notch people to be involved in the program.

RS: That's what I mean. If they brought in top-notch people, they'd blow the cover. So they have to go after people who are not top-notch and really don't know how to pursue this.

BL: That's a possibility, but I don't know.

GH: They could obviously get any top-notch physicist in there, if they'd allow him in, so the criteria must be something else.

ML: Do you know, and are you willing to say, how this program is funded?

BL: That I don't know. I heard — and I really don't remember if I read it or it was hearsay — that this was being funded through SDI. I really don't remember where I first heard that.

GH: There's an investigation going on right now with his W-2 that might shed some light on that subject.

RS: Is it true that you had MAJ on your identification badge? Did you actually see any Majestic insignia?

BL: Yes. There again, I cracked a smile immediately when I saw that, and I began to wonder, is this really the Majestic everyone talks about, or was it something done almost for nostalgia reasons? Assuming the Majestic-12 documents were false, did these guys just use this insignia for the hell of it, kind of as a joke? But my and everyone's badge said MAJ. The only person whose badge actually said Majestic on it was Dennis. I believe he was chief of security or something along those lines. He was certainly not of a scientific caliber. He was never involved in any of the physics. But any time there was trouble, Dennis was there. In fact, they once had kind of a covert meeting down at one of the casinos, and I got Gene in there to see him, so it looked like we weren't together. Dennis even looks like a Marine. You know, kind of built. He didn't fit the mold.

ML: What's your sense? Is this the Majestic of mythology?

BL: That I don't know. But Majestic was certainly on Dennis's badge, and I was told that Majestic is the name of that clearance — 38 levels above Q clearance is Majestic clearance. Maybe someone did have that knowledge and expanded on it in their own mind and created an MJ-12 document. Or maybe that is MJ-12. Maybe that's who I worked for. You can speculate forever, but that's the extent of what I know.

RS: And then it appears on your W-2 form, and the challenge is to find out what that employee identification number is all about.

BL: Right, which is what we're currently doing.

ML: Do you know if any of the other saucers at S 4 were operational?

BL: I believe they were, but I don't know for a fact.

ML: There's talk that joint human-alien space projects have produced bases on the moon and even on Mars. Did you see any information at all that lends credibility to that talk?

BL: No.

ML: Is there any indication that you know of that human beings have flown this kind of craft into space?

BL: No. None whatsoever, and I don't think they would have risked it. I doubt very much that they're proficient enough to get it back, once it's in a zero-G environment. Specifically, they're not familiar with operating it in "Beta-mode." I know it's not really called Beta-mode, and for the past year I've been trying to remember what it's called, but I'm going to call it Beta-mode anyway. I think once they get into an area of low gravity, they have great difficulty operating the craft. As the craft begins its roll maneuver and gets up into a lower gravity situation, that's when you go into Beta-mode, and it's very difficult to operate from there. I think that's why they wanted to concentrate on that specific area. So no, I don't think they've left the planet.

GH: Also, looking at it logically, considering what the fuel is, what if it crashed, and what kind of a nuclear explosion might there be? How do they explain it if that happens? There are lots of reasons why they probably don't just go joy-riding.

ML: Could you actually get a nuclear explosion out of this thing?

BL: No, it's far too stable for that, though there'd be a localized explosion because there is active anti-matter in a small portion of the reactor, but not a lot. Depending at what power level the craft is being operated, I don't think there'd be very much of an explosion. And chances are, I think, in a crash situation most systems would shut down.

GH: The guys that cut one open did die from an explosion.

ML: Yes, but that doesn't take much of an explosion.

GH: Well, he could elaborate on the explosion a little bit, how it blew the blast door off into the monitoring area.

BL: That's true. It was a good bang, I'd say in the 20 kiloton range or something like that.

ML: That big? OK.

PH: Are we only talking about the sport model so far?

BL: That's the only thing I know about.

PH: What's the diameter of that?

BL: Thirty or 35 feet.

PH: And how much power is the reactor developing?

BL: A tremendous amount of power. I don't remember specifically, but...

PH: Megawatts?

BL: It was greater than megawatts. I seem to remember 100 or 200 megawatts.

ML: If you had some 115, knowing what you know, do you think you could recreate that reactor, or the amplifiers?

BL: The amplifiers, yes. The reactor's the only thing I have a problem with right now.

ML: You wouldn't know how to recreate the reactor?

BL: And have it operate under a controlled fashion? No. I can have it react, but...[laugh] The amplifier's a breeze. I can certainly do that, and I just don't know enough about the reactor to duplicate it, but I think in time I'll be able to.

ML: Without a device that propagates gravity waves, is that amplifier itself good for anything?

BL: No.

ML: Turning the question around again, do you know how to propagate gravity waves in a controlled way?

BL: Yes, I do.

PH: Perhaps there's a less efficient way of doing it...

BL: I believe there was a test using plutonium. I think this is part of the Cash-Landrum UFO incident [see Briefing], where this was actually done, and there was a large quantity of plutonium specifically for that purpose.

ML: Are you suggesting that the flying machine associated with the Cash-Landrum incident was human-built,

BRIEFING:

The Cash-Landrum Incident

At around 9 pm on December 29, 1980, three people witnessed an unusual aircraft fly over State Road 1485 near Dayton, Texas, not far from Houston. Betty Cash, Vickie Landrum and Vickie's young grandson Colby were driving home when they noticed a bright light in the sky ahead. Betty, the driver, stopped in the road when the light became almost blinding, then got out of the car to get a better view as the craft hovered only a few hundred feet away. The craft seemed roughly diamond-shaped, narrow at the bottom and broader above. Flames issued from the bottom, accompanied by an intermittant roaring noise. The heat and light were intense.

Returning to the car, Betty found the door handle too hot to touch. The three witnesses were all very frightened, but they continued watching from their car as the craft moved slowly away from the road. Moments later, they also saw more than twenty large, twin-rotor helicopters (later identified as Army Chinooks) flying nearby, as if to escort the strange craft. They arrived home at approximately 9:45 pm.

By morning, all three developed physical symptoms later attributed to acute radiation poisoning. Betty's were the worst, including severe headache, nausea, oozing skin sores and hair loss. After four days of intense suffering, she was admitted to the hospital for observation and treatment, where she remained for six weeks. Her doctors could not account for her condition, but Betty and several independent investigators express certainty that her contact with the strange aircraft was the cause. In recent years, Betty has developed cancer, and all three witnesses have had continuous health problems.

The presence of Army helicopters convinced Betty and Vickie that the craft belonged to the U.S. military. On that basis, they sued the government for $20 million in damages for exposing them to radiation. They were interviewed by military personnel at Bergstrom Air Force Base, but were never offered any explanations or assistance. In August, 1986, their lawsuit was dismissed from U.S. District Court following testimony by military and NASA officials that no such craft was owned or operated by the government.

What did Betty Cash and Vickie and Colby Landrum actually encounter? Other witnesses confirm that a large number of Chinook-type helicopters were operating in their area that evening in 1980. Independent investigator John Schuessler went to the scene seven weeks after the original sighting and took photos of a large blackened area on the road that could have been caused by intense heat from above. A few weeks later, Schuessler says, a team of workers with unmarked machinery dug up and replaced that entire section of road. Judging from their severe medical problems, Betty, Vickie and Colby encountered intense radiation where none should have been, and there is little reason to doubt their testimony that it came from an unconventional aircraft. If so, was this an experimental vehicle of human manufacture? Was it an alien craft being tested by the military? To date, the questions remain unanswered. — ML

powered by plutonium, using this kind of technology?

BL: Yes, that's exactly what I'm suggesting. Supposedly — now, this wasn't in documentation that I read, but I've seen it surface several times, and I believe I heard some reference to it — there is a craft buried out at Area 51 somewhere that was heavily contaminated, and I think that was another test of a plutonium-powered vehicle. But I think the amount of plutonium we're talking about is certainly a dangerous amount to be hauling around in a craft. It would be very difficult to contain, and I think it's a very inefficient fuel for what they're doing.

PH: Do you have to use some nuclear bombardment to produce the gravitational wave?

BL: No. It may enhance it or amplify it to some degree, or stimulate it to produce more. But just a single piece of 115 lying on the table has a sufficient enough gravitational wave to deflect a laser fired over it.

I don't know if I mentioned it before, but the amplifiers always run at 100 percent. They are always outputting a maximum gravity wave, and that wave is phase-shifted from zero to 180 degrees. That's essentially the attraction and repulsion, and it's normally at a null setting somewhere in between. It's a very straight-forward system. It looks more like a coal fired engine than very hi-tech. People claim that this technology is tens of thousands of years ahead of us. I think the reality is that this technology is probably around one hundred or two hundred years ahead of us.

RS: Bob, you said you read in the document room some rather strange references to human evolution and the aliens' role in human genetics. How did that come up, in what context? What was it you saw?

BL: I hate to repeat this stuff. I say this every time I mention it, because I have no other proof that it's true, other than the fact that I read it; and I always follow that up by saying, yes, everything I read about the propulsion system turned out to be fact. But it's really far-fetched, and even though I did work with alien technology on flying saucers, I still find it difficult to come to grips with the physical alien thing in itself. But as far as where that came from, yes, there was a book that was almost like a history of the development of the human race. It was written from a different point of view. I don't think that particular thing had a title to it. But that's where we were referred to as "containers." Any time the word "human" came up, it was always replaced with the word "containers." Earth was referred to as Sol 3 instead of earth. It was a strangely written report.

ML: What do you think the word "containers" referred to?

BL: That referred to people. Now, containers of what, I don't know. You can speculate on that until you turn blue.

ML: This book you're referring to — are you saying this book was of alien origin?

BL: I'll tell you exactly how it looked. It was certainly odd, in that it was written from another point of view. It was like a history book of us, like someone had been looking at the earth and written a brief history of what had happened, and how everything living here looked, so on and so forth. If you remember the old Collier's Encyclopedias, in the section on anatomy they had the clear pages that you could turn, and there's the circulatory system, the organs, and so forth. OK. This was one of the most fascinating things in the briefings, other than the information itself. As you turned the page — it would be a picture of, for instance, an adobe house — and as you moved the page up, you'd see through the different levels of the house, almost like those little 3-D things you bend and see different views, but it was very smooth and clear, much higher resolution. I'd just never seen anything like that. I don't know if it actually exists anywhere, or if we're talking about something of alien origin, but as you turn the page, you can see the superstructure, and then down to the wood itself, then the foundation. It was fascinating. That's how all the illustrations were. There again, there were no references to people. Everything was "containers."

ML: But it was clear from the context that the word container referred to people? [BL: Right.] What kinds of things did they say about the people? Did they talk about how people behave, what the historical development was?

BL: What they were talking about was the desirability of containers, and that the containers were not damaged. Now, people speculate on containers. Are they talking about containers of souls, something bizarre like that; or is it the opposite? Is the container the soul, and it contains the body? That's too far out really for me to grasp, but they were talking about the preservation of the containers, and how unique they are. Extremely, extremely unique...

GH: That life like ours was very difficult to find.

BL: Very difficult to find.

BL: By the way, the book, if flipped over, is two books put together. One's upside down. This way, it's kind of the basic history of earth. You flip it over and read it the other way, and it has to do with Reticulum Four, as they called it, which dealt with the alien civiliation.

ML: So that book contained, in effect, a history of the earth from an alien perspective. Is that correct? [BL: Right.] And then, on the other hand, an alleged history or perspective on Reticulum Four, which presumably is the planet that these...

BL: Right, that's as stated in the book. But of course, I can't attest to the validity of the information in there. Unfortunately, when I first opened the book the way it was sitting, and was playing with the pages and the drawings in there, it was some time before I realized what was on the flip side of it. So I wasted a lot of time reading about the earth history. When I flipped it over, I realized it had to do with a lot of the alien civilization. Maybe I could have learned a lot more there.

Still, on top of all that, even with photographs of autopsies and aliens, that was certainly NOT what I was interested in. Yes, it's fascinating and awe-inspiring, but I really wanted hardware.

GH: People ask Bob, do you think it was disinformation? But the information is so extensive that it just seems inconceivable that someone could have made this up.

ML: The photographs sound rather difficult to reproduce, except by some odd technology.

BL: Having a photo lab, that's what intrigued me and why I played with it for so long.

ML: Had you ever seen anything like that? Are you aware of anything that can do that?

BL: No. It was like a mylar-based page, and it was almost a clear section where the picture was. It changed, but it didn't change in steps, like most diffraction-grating, 3-D looking pictures do.

PH: How do you feel, emotionally speaking, with the fairly certain knowledge that extra-terrestrial beings are out there, and they've visited the earth, and they're probably still coming around, and so on. Does it bother you at all?

BL: No, it's the only thing that makes sense. It takes a lot of the confusion out of things. A lot more knits together, and now things begin to make complete sense.

PH: Don't you feel — no pun intended — don't you feel alienated? In fact, aren't you kind of connected with them, and removed from the rest of society that doesn't accept that?

BL: Absolutely. I feel like I really know what's going on, and everyone's an idiot. I really do feel that way. Alienated is the perfect word for it.

PH: Does it make you feel lonely and isolated?

BL: No, because I don't think I'm the only one who believes that...

PH: But you're one of the few people who know it...

BL: Yes.

PH: I was curious, because I go through that myself as I become more or less convinced that this is what's going on. I try to go over what that does to my relationship with the rest of society...

BL: It really just pushes you away from it. And it becomes increasingly impossible to convince anyone of the truth.

GH: But you have to expose people to it. I'm certain that even the people in this room, all of us, at some point in time were exposed to it enough and did enough investigation to where this makes sense. Now you understand it, and actually, reality makes much more sense than all the things we've made up. So, I think before we call everyone else idiots, everyone should have the right to be exposed to it. And then if they ignore it, I think you could designate them as idiots if you want, but there are a lot of good, intelligent people who've had no cause to think much about it.

RS: What was your attitude about extraterrestrials before you got involved with this program?

BL: I was the greatest skeptic of all time. In fact, it was almost a year before, I think, that a friend who later went to work up at Tonopah came to my house with an article cut out of the paper. He said, "Hey look, there's this guy named John Lear, and he's talking about aliens and the government down at the Spring Valley library. Do you want to go?" And I said, "You are a blithering idiot. Why would you even waste the time listening to this guy?" It was a big joke. And then, again, he said, "I just came back from there, and I can't even get in. The place is packed." I just thought it was ridiculous. Now I always look back at that, because I remember, though I had nothing to stand on, that I was firmly convinced, and it annoyed me that he even believed that this was possible. It just shows me how close-minded I was.

ML: You and nearly everyone else. I think we can all look to our own example. I too was closed to it, until a certain kind of information came my way that I felt I could no longer ignore. And the minute you open to it and start looking, you see that there's a tremendous amount of information out there. But there's seemingly a threshold a person has to cross before they are able to see that information.

BL: And you'll continue to fight it along the way, too. The day I got off the bus at S 4 and walked into the hangar, and as soon as I saw the edge of the sport model, the edge of the craft, it was kind of an overwhelming feeling. But immediately I thought, this explains all the UFO stuff. We made them, and they've just been testing it, and, you know... There's an alien craft in front of my face, and I caught myself making excuses right there. I was immediately denying it. Of course, I didn't sleep that night. In fact, I think I saw Gene the next day, and I came in, my eyes were red, and he said, "Bob, are you OK? What happened?" But that night, lying in bed, I remember just giggling, that right at that moment when I walked by and slid my hand on it, I'm trying to think of other possibilities, and purposely shying away from, yes, it looks like a flying saucer, but... The clincher was looking inside.

RS: You've mentioned seeing "little furniture." When was that?

BL: That was when I first got off the bus. I purposely plotted my course to go by it so I could touch it. I think I touched it with my fingernail, because I wanted to make sure it wasn't cardboard or something, and this wasn't some sort of psychological test. But I felt it was obviously metal, and as I walked by I looked in there and could see that everything was very small. I was immediately told to keep looking forward. Obviously, they brought me through there to show me, or else they wouldn't have. But that first time I saw the craft was when I first saw the inside. It wasn't until much later that I actually got to go inside.

RS: How did that come about? What was it like to walk inside?

BL: Well, they really didn't want me inside. What they wanted me to see, and the only reason I went in, was to see the orientation of the gravity amplifiers. There are three levels to the disk. As you walk in the door, to the left and down, there's a panel that comes off, and you can go down to where the amplifiers hang. You really can't fit in there, you can squeeze your body in and lie upside down and see how things are. That was what they wanted me to do. There were other people working inside on the second level, the main level. The third level I never got to see. I have no idea what's up there. I imagine, or just guess, that maybe it's some sort of navigational equipment or something like that. You know, the bridge. Who knows? But, the intention was for me only to see what was down there, and I think they were waiting for a convenient time when nothing would be going on on the second level. But there really was no way to isolate me from the rest of the craft. So I was led in there.

There was a staircase going up to the side of the craft. The door was removed, or maybe a hole had been cut, I have no idea. But I was immediately directed to look down. The panel was taken off, and I kind of squeezed down there. It's such a small hole, obviously it wasn't made for a human to go poking around down there. But once you wedge in there, you're isolated and sealed off. It's kind of claustrophobic in there. That in itself was an ominous experience, because you can see...I can't even describe it...the amplifiers hanging down, and it just looks powerful and awesome. I don't know what else I can say. Right above that is where the reactor is. As I wedged my way out of there — I was brought in there by Barry, I believe — Barry's back was turned, and he was standing on the stairs looking down at other people around the craft. And of course, I came out and felt obliged to look around. So that's when I took the opportunity to do that, really quickly. There were other people diddling around some consoles. I call them consoles, but there was nothing on top of them. They were large boxes that were mounted to the second level of the craft. One of them obviously had been torn off by us. For the most part, it was basically empty in there.

RS: Had they taken everything out of there, do you think?

BL: I don't know.

GH: You know he's likened the sport model to one of the Billy Meier crafts, right? [To BL:] Didn't you tell me that when you were right up next to it, it's taller and you don't get the sensation of it being so sleek, and it wasn't until you saw it fly that you noticed it looked like the Meier photo?

BL: It doesn't look anything like that Meier photo when you're up close. It looks proportionately different, because it looks too tall. It looks pregnant, more or less. It doesn't look nearly as sleek looking right from the rim upward. It just looked like a basic, science-fiction movie flying saucer. It didn't look special at all. Certainly it looked all molded, with no seams. Even the seats as they're connected to the floor, everything was molded or cast, every last piece of it. How that was done, I don't know.

PH: The extraterrestrials sometimes seem to speak with some kind of telepathic communication. I'm wondering if you have any ideas about that.

BL: I'm not entirely convinced that it's a biological system in itself.

PH: Do you think they have a little transducer or something?

BL: Yes, I do.

RS: Let me clarify. In other words, telepathy is a technological development on their part?

BL: I believe so.

RS: Was there documentation that suggested this was the case?

BL: I believe there was mention of telepathy. As far as why I think it's a non-biological function, that's just my own personal opinion. That really has no basis. But if I remember, there was mention of some sort of psionic abilities.

RS: Any mention of implants? Abductions?

BL: No. Nothing with abductions, nothing with cattle.

ML: How about genetic hybridization?

BL: The only mention of anything genetic in relation to humans was that there were apparently 65, or maybe 63, instances of what they called externally corrected evolution — 65 or 63 genetic alterations made along the development of the human race.

ML: Are you saying that in the report you read, there was a specific reference to 65 or 63 genetic alterations, presumably made by an alien race upon the human race to affect the whole race?

BL: Yes, upon a simian being, not even a purely human character.

ML: Were these alterations, then, the alterations which resulted in Homo sapiens, ourselves?

BL: Right. That was in that one odd book that I mentioned.

ML: Was there any indication of when these alterations occurred, even a rough time-frame?

BL: No. There were mentioned events in excess of 10,000 years old, but...

ML: Presumably, if we're talking about the genetic alteration of a simian being, we're talking a long, long time ago.

BL: Right. But as to how many millions of years we're talking about, there was no reference to it, at least that I remember.

PH: Did you see any photographs of longer ago than we have photographs?

BL: No.

GH: Did you read that it was a simian being, or are you just saying it was so long ago that simian is your term?

BL: Simian is my term. I try to remember it verbatim, but it's been so long ago...

PH: [to GH]: Gene, how do you feel about all this? Does it disturb you?

GH: No, not really. Before, we didn't even know what the questions are. It's more comforting to know at least that much now. What do you think the ramifications are, if we're externally corrected evolution, and if they've been coming around for a long time? Where do you think it's going to lead? It's going to lead right to religious values, right to the basic questions that bother man: who are we, where do we come from, where are we going to, life after death, God. Isn't that at the basis of it all? And that's where it leads you. In other words, it's going to make people face reality. And you know, that's a thing we don't do very well. We ignore reality — that's the thing we do best.

ML: I'm wondering how Bob would say that. Bob, you had the first-hand experience. What's your outlook on what this all means for the future of the human race?

BL: I'm skeptical of everything that I just read. I do tend to believe essentially what Gene said, but I just remain skeptical. It's as if you reach a different level when you've had contact with the information and actually experienced and related to some of the technology. It just takes more now to convince me of something. See, you really can't reach that level, or enter that type of belief system, because whether it's something that you read from a different source or that I tell you, it's always hearsay. Yet, I went into a different stage, essentially, where now it's reality as well as hearsay. Once you've stepped into the reality category, you tend to push everything else away and say, OK, this isn't real unless I touched it. That's why I put a lot less credit into just the printed word. Do I believe we're the product of an alien civilization tinkering with genes? Maybe. That's the best I can say.

PH: In the last couple of years, there's been a tremendous increase in acceptance about the idea of extraterrestrials. I've been hearing about it since I was a kid, because my father became interested in the UFO sightings back in the 1940s. But it seems to me that in the last couple of years, there's been a tremendous amount of varying information coming forward, and more and more, it's being acknowledged.

BL: I think what's happening is that the damage in their veil of secrecy is cumulative. What I mean is that with every little crack or nudge, some information leaks out and stays there. Disinformation or whatever doesn't heal it up. Now I think there are so many cracks and leaks, so much is dribbling out, and it's being taken up by the media on a little more serious stance than it used to be, that pretty soon it's almost going to be a fad, the way I see it happening. The ball is starting to roll, and I think it's certainly not going to roll and then stop. It's just becoming increasingly accepted. And it's really paving the way to where there's going to be a point — I wouldn't say the information is just going to be dumped out on the public — but there must be some sort of plan somewhere in the works or that's already operating, maybe that I'm part of, to have this information released.

Editor's Note: In April of 1991, shortly before this book went to press, Ralph Steiner and I began interviewing a number of people whose eyewitness testimony could substantiate many elements of Bob Lazar's story. We began developing our contacts with these people in mid-1990. Some of them have held very high security clearances and claim to have worked inside facilities operated jointly by military and alien personnel. The claimed locations of these facilities are not in Nevada. We anticipate speaking with other witnesses before making our findings public; but if the trend of our evidence continues, it would indicate that the alleged projects at S 4 are only a small part of a much larger pattern. — ML

Budd Hopkins

Chapter Four
Budd Hopkins: The Case for Abduction

Budd Hopkins was born in 1931 in West Virginia. After graduating from Oberlin College in 1953, he moved to New York City, where he has resided ever since. He is a painter and sculptor whose works are included in the permanent collections of the Whitney, Guggenheim and Hirshhorn Museums, the Museum of Modern Art, the Carnegie-Mellon, the Brooklyn Museum and many others. He has been awarded fellowships by both the Guggenheim Foundation and the National Endowment for the Arts, and his articles on painting and sculpture have appeared in America's major art magazines.

Budd's interest in UFOs began with a personal sighting in 1964, but his activities as a researcher began in 1975 when, at the urging of an elderly friend, he investigated a reported UFO landing in New Jersey. Before long, he decided to focus on cases of alleged alien abduction. With his 1981 publication of the landmark study *Missing Time*, Budd established himself as one of the world's foremost authorities on the abduction phenomenon. His second book, *Intruders: The Incredible Visitations at Copley Woods*, published in 1987, caused a worldwide sensation with its documented claim that alien abductions are leading to the creation of alien-human hybrids on earth. "The central focus of the entire UFO phenomenon is the study and laboratory use of human beings, with special attention to our physical, genetic and reproductive properties," he says.

A key element in Budd's approach to abduction from the beginning has been his reliance on the expert help of psychiatrists, psychologists and hypnotherapists. Though skeptics have criticized his methodology as well as his findings, a growing number of mental-health professionals attest to the legitimacy of his work. Many others, following his lead, have investigated abduction cases of their own, with similar results.

In 1989, Budd established the Intruders Foundation (IF) in order to handle the ever-increasing requests for information and assistance from abductees and others concerned about the abduction phenomenon. Budd's vision for IF includes a referral service to psychotherapists nationwide who are specially trained to work with abductees; a data bank to assist serious research on abduction; and a speakers bureau and other educational services to raise public awareness about this phenomenon. IF is a not-for-profit foundation staffed by volunteers and supported mainly by private contributions. Those wishing to learn more can write to: The Intruders Foundation, P.O. Box 30233, New York, NY 10011.

I met Budd Hopkins on November 1, 1990, when he consented to the following face-to-face interview while in Santa Barbara for a UFO conference. I found him to be a gracious and charming man, passionately devoted to the abductees he works with and deeply concerned about the fate of humanity. — ML

Michael Lindemann: Budd, how long have you been investigating the UFO phenomenon, and what prompted you to get started?

Budd Hopkins: My interest in the subject preceded my doing any investigation by eleven years. I got interested in the subject in 1964. At that time I had no interest or knowledge of the subject whatsoever. But I had a daylight sighting of a UFO over Cape Cod, together with two other people, my former wife and a house guest. That sighting lasted about three minutes, and we were clearly looking at a metallic craft which was circular, which could hover and zoom off silently at great speed. We eventually stopped the car and got out to look at the thing as it passed the car behind us and went out to sea. But the point is, suddenly I was aware that there was an object, a craft, flying around which obviously tended to support all the reports that had been made over the years, that I had not paid any attention to. And I suddenly thought, there's something going on here that needs looking into.

So I began in 1964 to just read about it, and had no further serious interest except informing myself about the material. Of course, the more I read about it, the more I realized that the Air Force explanations — that these were balloons or something — looked totally ridiculous. And I realized we were facing a genuine mystery which could be, if it were true, the most important event in all of human history.

If you get curious about whether or not there's another kind of fish swimming around in a lake in Scotland, and that fish is found, we have another fish. But in this issue, if this is a legitimate intrusion into our world by some other kind of intelligence with an incredibly developed technology, it's not just another fish in a Scottish lake. This is the biggest event, the most portentious kind of news that one could imagine. It's very hard to let something like that alone.

I got seriously involved in investigating in 1975, because an elderly man that I'd known for quite a while told me, with a lot a fear, about something that zoomed alongside his car in a park in New Jersey. It stopped ahead of his car, and it was a 35-foot disk. As he approached it, little figures got out and started digging soil samples. The man was 60 feet away from a group of UFO occupants, absolutely terrified. And I knew one of two things. Either he had done a lot of careful research to get the details right in a hoaxed story, which I had no reason to believe, because this man is not a reader and he didn't know that I was even curious about the subject; or he was describing exactly what had happened. I went back to the site with him, and we found physical evidence. I did my first investigation there. I located a second witness who'd seen the whole thing from another point of view. That man, luckily for all of us, had reported to the police, so we had reports that we could date to that night.

The UFO was described as having an odd color, nothing that we get in reports. It was described by both the witnesses, who of course had no knowledge of one another, as black. So,

when I wrote a long article about this for the *Village Voice*[1]—
there were many other aspects of the case that were interesting
— I withheld the color of the craft and one other detail, because
I wanted to try to smoke out any other witnesses who might
have seen this thing that night and be able to check their
veracity by these hidden details. We got something like five
more witnesses. At that point, I was beginning to hear from a
lot of other people about their cases, because they had read
about my investigation in the *Village Voice*. It was also reprinted
other places, including *Cosmopolitan* magazine and some
newspapers.

I began to get accounts which had pieces of missing time
in the description, things about which I knew enough to
recognize as part of an abduction pattern. But when I was doing
this in 1975 and '76, abductions were something that I had only
reluctantly come to accept, through the Betty and Barney Hill
case. In 1975, we only had about three abduction cases that the
public was aware of — the Hill case; Pascagoula, Mississippi
[see Briefing]; and the Travis Walton case — and it was the
furthest thing from anybody's mind that these things might be
common. But the more people contacted me, the more I found
these pieces of missing time connected with their reports, and
overtones of an abduction experience. So I began to get very
curious about that, and thanks to a psychiatrist, a psychologist
and other investigators, all working as a team, we began to
uncover one after another of these cases. That led to what I
consider the most important discovery I've made all along, and
that is that these events are conceivably extremely common,
rather than rare.

ML: You've mentioned the phenomenon of missing time as one
of the things that alerted you to the abduction possibility.
Explain what missing time is. How does it work?

BH: In the Betty and Barney Hill case, the most famous, classic
case, the Hills remembered a gap in the continuity of their
story. They remember that they stopped their car, that they got

BRIEFING

The Pascagoula Abduction

When the United States Air Force shut down Project Blue Book in 1969, they evidently hoped the UFO phenomenon would quietly fade from public awareness. For a few years, that seemed to be the case. But on October 11, 1973, an event occurred that rekindled UFO interest nationwide.

Charles Hickson, age 42, and Calvin Parker, age 19, both of Gautier, Mississippi, were fishing that evening from a pier along the Pascagoula River. Darkness had fallen and the two men were about to return to Hickson's car, parked a few hundred feet away. Suddenly, blue lights started strobing in the dark. They heard a hissing sound, then saw the outline of a strange object that seemed to hover just above the ground nearby. An opening appeared in the object, through which they first saw a bright light, then three odd beings floating toward them about two feet off the ground. Two beings reached for Hickson, one on each arm, and floated him into the craft. One being reached for Parker, who evidently fainted as he was escorted to the lighted opening.

During their time inside the object, neither man knew the whereabouts of the other. Hickson says he found Parker standing on the riverbank as if in a trance, and shook him awake following his own release. Under separate questioning by local police that night, the two men gave similar descriptions of the craft and the beings, and Hickson remembered many details of his time on board, though Parker could not. Their accounts were later reinforced by hypnotic regression, and Hickson underwent and passed a polygraph test.

Hickson and Parker said their abductors were a little over five feet tall, with elongated heads, no necks, long arms ending in mitten-like pincers, and legs that never moved and seemed locked together. They had gray skin that ran in heavy horizontal folds around their bodies — like elephant skin, Hickson thought. Their heads had three pointed protrusions that could have been nose and ears, and slits that seemed to be mouths. Heavy folds of skin on their foreheads left Hickson and Parker unsure if the beings had eyes. Hickson later said he thought the beings might be robots, because their movements seemed stiff and mechanical.

The craft itself was described as elliptical in shape, about thirty feet in length and fifteen feet high, with a slight dome on top. Hickson thought the opening was a sliding door about six feet in height. The exterior blue lights of the craft glowed only during its arrival and departure, but its interior

continued next page

illumination was so blinding that Hickson could not make out any features except a TV-like screen on one wall.

Once inside, Hickson found he was completely paralyzed. He tried to speak, but could not hear his own voice. He remained in a standing position while being examined by a free-floating "eye" that looked like a crystal sphere with a smaller metallic ball rotating inside it. This "eye" scanned his body top to bottom, front and back, then disappeared from view. Hickson later surmised that this examination was the main purpose of his abduction. Shortly afterward, he was escorted back outside by two beings, where he found Parker. Both men then saw the craft glow bright blue, rise very suddenly into the air and disappear.

Hickson and Parker both felt terrified and confused, but quickly decided to report their experience to the authorities. Within hours of their alleged abduction, they gave lengthy statements to the local sheriff, and the next morning were tested for radiation and interrogated by military personnel at Keesler Air Force Base in nearby Biloxi. Both men insisted they did not want publicity, but the sheriff's office leaked their story to the press and caused an instant uproar. Within 12 hours, Hickson and Parker were besieged by reporters. The story made headlines nationwide.

The case attracted the attention of two top UFO researchers, Dr. James Harder and Dr. J. Allen Hynek, both of whom were on the scene within 36 hours. On October 13, Hynek issued a statement to the press, saying: "'There's simply no question in my mind that these men have had a very real, frightening experience...under no circumstances should these men be ridiculed. They are absolutely honest. They have had a fantastic experience."

Hickson and Parker seemed physically unharmed by their ordeal. Hickson reported a sharp pain in his left shoulder when the beings first grabbed him, then noticed the next day that he had an inexplicable bleeding sore on his left arm; but this sore soon disappeared. Hickson later said of his alleged abductors, "It was like they had a job to do, and they did it and left." In recent years, he has spoken freely about his encounter, saying that if it were to happen again, he would not be as frightened as he was in 1973.

Calvin Parker, however, was apparently more upset than Hickson by whatever really happened on the Pascagoula River. One month after his encounter, Parker suffered a nervous breakdown and was briefly hospitalized. He was later hospitalized again for treatment of stress and avoids public inquiry into his experience.

Hickson has published his own story in a book co-written with William Mendez, titled UFO Contact at Pascagoula (1983). Interested readers can write to him at 2024 Carol Drive, Gautier, MS 39553. — ML

out, that Barney was looking through binoculars at an object
that was landing, and that he ran back to the car because he saw
faces in the craft looking back at him. The very next recollection
they had was of being on the road, driving along home. They
didn't even remember getting in and starting the car. Now,
obviously, if you're frightened, you might have a little confusion as to what you do, but you're certainly going to remember
the panic of starting the car, trying to back up and turn around
and get on the highway and so forth. It was extremely strange
to them, as well as to everybody they told the story to, that there
was this missing piece in the continuity of the narrative. Then
they realized that they had literally lost a couple of hours that
they could not account for. And, as we now know, by the use
of hypnosis, they were able to recall what occurred during that
missing period of time.

In the cases that I was looking into, we were finding all of
these overtones, except that the subjects did not consciously
remember even seeing a UFO, which of course led them *not* to
think of their cases as connected with the UFO phenomenon.
For example, in 1974 a woman and her husband were driving
from the Jersey Shore, where they'd spent the weekend, back to
northern New Jersey where they lived. It was Sunday afternoon around 5:00 or so. They were driving along the highway,
and everything was normal. And for both of them, the very
next instant, it was nighttime. There was no sense of time
having passed. Just suddenly, it was night. It's as if someone
had a film of a person walking and snipped out the middle
section, so the person from one frame to the next jumps from
one side of the field to the other — it's that kind of effect in the
mind. So, it's nighttime; and they're in a field, in their car. The
lights are out. The motor is off. And they look at each other.
What the hell happened?

Now, mind you, they hadn't sighted anything. All they
knew is that they weren't even on a road. They had to start up
the car, and they bounced over this field before they found a
dirt road that led out of the field to a larger highway, which led
back to the main highway. And, of course, for weeks they went

through all kinds of self-doubt. Are we crazy? What happened? How could this have occurred to both of us? How did we get into this crazy field? And, of course, what happened to the four or five hours that obviously disappeared between a sunny afternoon and nighttime? Then came periods of anxiety attacks, such fear in the husband's case that he actually had to be taken to the emergency room and sedated. He didn't know what the source of the anxiety was.

Everything points to the fact that something big occurred in the lives of these two people during their missing time period. But in 1974, in most people's minds, a UFO event was essentially a sighting of something, an object. No one looked upon these subjective experiences as even remotely connected with UFOs. We know now that the sighting itself may be completely blanked out of the experience, a kind of enforced amnesia which seems to accompany abductions, as if the abductors are able to cancel out periods of memory, so that the person simply cannot remember what happened from a certain instant to another instant. And it's very interesting, in cases involving six or seven people, as some of them do, that their memories generally all turn off at the same moment and turn back on at the same moment.

At any rate, when one looks into this through careful questioning, and ultimately, if it's necessary, hypnotic regression, out comes the period of missing time in all its glory, all of the experiences that these people have undergone. That includes the sighting of the craft, the sighting of the figures being taken inside the craft, put on a table, the physical examination that takes place, and so forth. So, when I discovered this whole underside of the iceberg, as one might call it, that these events could be extremely common, I wrote a book about it, which I called *Missing Time*.[2] And that, of course, elicited many, many more cases. It's been a dramatic unfolding ever since.

ML: Do you think missing time is a factor in all abductions, or do you have cases where there's no sign of it?

BH: I think we have a spectrum here, a range of amnesia, let's say. There's a range from virtually total amnesia, where the person remembers absolutely nothing, to the other extreme where people have remembered their experiences the way you would remember an automobile accident or a mugging, virtually total recall from beginning to end. I have cases which would suggest that people were abducted, although they don't have even any funny feelings about it. But they were being searched for, for hours, in places where they couldn't possibly have disappeared. In one case, the person was supposed to be on guard duty in the Army. Later, when the people who were searching asked these people where they had gone, they just didn't know what had happened. They only knew they were missing because they were told by others that they were missing.

There are many variations in between — partial recollections, flashbacks. In one particular case, a woman from Argentina had an abduction of which she had no conscious memory at all, except a missing time situation and the sense of having seen an odd little figure that frightened her. She was a child at the time. She was scolded by her parents when she came home. They'd been searching for her, but she had no recollection of what had happened. Under hypnosis, it turned out to be a full-fledged, typical abduction experience. But this same woman, in her twenties, had an abduction experience which she remembers literally from beginning to end, consciously. When she was returned to her bedroom and was suddenly able to move, and the little people who had abducted her left, she shook her boyfriend and woke him up, and they spent the rest of the night talking about all of her recollections, writing everything down and making drawings. We've done a hypnotic recall of that experience, and virtually nothing important surfaced through hypnosis that she had not already recalled consciously.

So, it doesn't seem to be an exact science, if you want to put it that way. It's either something that would imply less than 100% skill on the abductors' part, or this is the way they want it to be. Or, perhaps, there's some other unknown factor which would cause certain people to remember more of experience A than experience B.

ML: So-called screen memory plays a role in many abductions. What's your current understanding of what that is?

BH: My current understanding of a screen memory is that it is something that is imposed deliberately on the abductee from the outside. Now, a screen memory in classical Freudian terms actually describes a situation in which a person who undergoes a traumatic event, let's say a rape, blocks it out of their mind. To make the event more palatable, or something they can live with, their own mind will provide a "cover story" for what really happened. That may operate in UFO cases, too. But we also have the sense, without any doubt, that these things are externally imposed.

   I'll give you an example. Two women were driving back from a party in Washington. They were in a warehouse district, and they remember coming upon a six-car pile-up, six wrecked cars, all of which had their lights on. But they were very surprised to see that there was no one there at all. There were no people in the cars, there were no injured, there were no police, there were no spectators, there were no fire trucks, nothing. And this was a fairly deserted intersection, about two in the morning.

   The two women went home, having lost a couple of hours they could not account for, and pondered why they hadn't stopped at this wreck. They pondered why they hadn't called the police. And they talked about this weird event with their friends and parents — they were college students at the time. A six-car pile-up doesn't occur without spectators, injuries and so forth. It's a rarity anyway, but how could it occur in a deserted area of Washington, DC, in the middle of the night? It took them a long time to begin wondering whether they had actually seen a six-car pile-up.

   One of the women had begun exploring her UFO abduction memories, and in that context mentioned the six-car pile-up to me. I worked with both women. Under hypnosis, it appeared that one was abducted and the other one wasn't, but that both had the same crazy, impossible scenario-explanation played into their heads. It gave them a kind of excuse for why they were late. But, of course, a six-car pile-up in the middle of nowhere, with them not stopping and nobody there, makes no sense. So, I think from that you can certainly infer the idea that these memories are played in from the outside.

ML: Let's go on a slightly different tack here. Some critics of your work argue that there are prosaic explanations for the phenomena that you attribute to abduction. These explanations might run the gamut from repressed rape or incest incidents all the way to nefarious CIA mind-control, such as John Marks and Martin Cannon have described.[3] How do you respond to that?

BH: The basic point is, with every kind of so-called blanket explanation, the explanation has to take care of all the cases, or at least the vast majority of them, or it doesn't work. In other words, any theory that only explains some of the data is not a tenable theory. It has to deal with the data very effectively. One of the problems is that you have two different kinds of players in this whole crazy business. One is the field investigators, the people who are actually out there talking to people who've had these experiences, myself included, who are really approaching things in a very pragmatic way. We're listening to what people tell us, and looking into what evidence there is to buttress those accounts. On the other hand, there are the theoreticians, who sit at home reading reports and wracking their brains for some kind of possible explanation, trying to counter different aspects of it without wanting to bother themselves to actually look into a case. Some of these theories are absolutely absurd.

You mentioned Cannon, who is talking about the whole thing as a CIA or government mind-control experiment. To explain the data, he would have to say that this was developed by Calvin Coolidge, say, or at least in his administration, because the earliest cases that I have, classic abduction cases, are two from 1929. And if you want to slip back in time to Calvin Coolidge's presidency for the development of this, at that time, as we all remember, crystal radio sets were about as far as we'd gone. I have hundreds and hundreds of cases from the 1930's and 1940's. You then have to assume that, whoever these nefarious souls are who were doing this to people, they were able to do it simultaneously in New Zealand and Zimbabwe and places like that, and that they were busy putting implants in the brains of dentists in New Jersey in 1936.

Now, I have no doubt that the CIA is doing all kinds of ghastly and disgusting things. A friend of mine named Eric Olsen lost his father, who was a CIA employee, to a CIA experiment with LSD. He was fed the drug without his knowledge, and he leapt out the window of a hotel, believing that he could fly. This was a very famous case. I'm the first one to condemn this sort of CIA experimentation. But, my actual guess is that the CIA, or some government agency, knowing about the widespread abduction phenomenon — and I'm certain of the government cover-up — has probably been madly trying to develop some kind of technology, at least since the 1960's, based on what they've been hearing about from UFO accounts.

So, I think that Cannon has probably stumbled into an intelligence area that's playing a game of cover-up, and catch-up, with what's been going on in the UFO field. It's a totally absurd theory. The CIA would have to be running around implanting hundreds of thousands of people with gadgets in their heads. The whole thing makes no sense. The other theories don't hold water either. This is a situation, it seems to me, where a straight line turns out to be the shortest distance between two points. These people are just describing what's happened to them, and the physical kinds of evidence that we have support the stories exactly as they deliver them.

ML: You've mentioned implants several times. There's a lot of talk that implants figure large in the abduction phenomenon. But what hard evidence do you have that these implants are actually there?

BH: I'm going to duck this question right now. Let me just say that we're doing some investigations right now which are extremely interesting. I'm opposed to making any claims at all until we have absolute clarity of scientific opinion about certain issues. We're just at the early stage of approaching that kind of clarity of thinking. In other words, it's an area of evidence that's extremely rich and interesting right now, which I'd rather not talk about.

ML: Would you mind explaining how hypnosis figures in your work? How often do you use it, and how important is it in the collection of your data?

BH: We know that if a person has seen an automobile accident or a crime being committed, hypnosis can elicit more details. It helps flesh out the evidence of that particular event, because a lot of things are simply forgotten, and this is a way of helping people remember certain things. There's probably no abduction account that we have where you could say that every single bit of information has been consciously recalled. Most people remember large pieces of their experiences. But they may not remember inside the craft, on-the-table experiences as fully as they remember the beginnings or the endings of their experiences. Hypnosis seems to be particularly useful because we have no doubt that there is a period of amnesia in the people who are reporting. The way we use hypnosis seems to be akin to the way it's used to block the memories to start with. It's almost as if we're using the same key to unlock the memories that the UFO occupants have used to lock them up.

It doesn't make any difference, incidentally, who does the hypnosis. I've worked with all kinds of psychiatrists, psychologists, skeptics. It doesn't make any difference who's doing the hypnosis, the accounts that come out are exactly the same. It's just a technical procedure to relax the person, to allow their memories to come to the top. What's recalled is not a function of the hypnotist.

To return to one of your questions about what skeptics say: One of the theories is that people were the victims of child abuse or whatever, and this is a cover story they've invented. Actually, at this point, I've worked with four psychiatrists who are themselves abductees, who've come to me for hypnosis because of their own experiences. I'm about to work with a fifth. And I've worked with five psychologists and numerous psychotherapists who have had these experiences. I've had many therapists and mental health professionals refer people to me who were their own clients or patients, but who these therapists recognized were recalling UFO experiences. So, we're talking about a huge number of cases that have been, as it were, endorsed by mental health professionals as being not something of normal origin. These are not child abuse cases or whatever. It's a handy thing to say, off the top of the head. Of course, probably 25% of the abductees *were* sexually abused children, if in fact 25% of the population as a whole were sexually abused as children. What we're getting amongst the abductees is clearly a cross-section of society. So, the percentage of homosexuals, the percentage of people with certain kinds of diseases, the percentage of people with childhood abuse problems and so forth is probably identical within the sample of abductees and the population as a whole.

ML: That raises an interesting question. Do you notice anything at all that typifies an abductee, that would suggest that certain people are more susceptible than others?

BH: You immediately get into the chicken-and-egg problem here, if you assume that abductions begin in the very earliest years of life. I've got a number of cases where something occurred in the hospital at the time of the baby's birth, suggesting contact within the first few days of life. If you assume that that child is now going to grow up to be regularly abducted, it's very hard to imagine that person as separate from these experiences — it just really can't be done.

There are certain things that I think I've learned to recognize in people, and this is totally subjective, probably indefensible. But at any rate, I would say that most abductees that I've worked with have an immediately more open, broader attitude toward every kind of metaphysical, spiritual question or possibility. They are not necessarily people who respect authority automatically, by rote. In a strange way, they have seen a larger universe, closer up, than most of us have, whether they remember it very clearly or not. As one person said, it's as if, especially when they begin exploring their experiences, they've gotten rid of the tunnel vision that most people have suffered from.

On the other hand, I've never met anybody who I think was helped by this. The psychological scars are there for everybody. Often, in a room full of abductees at a support group meeting, I see a lot of extremely attractive, interesting, intelligent people, and I realize that there are very, very few successful relationships in that room amongst the people. It's tougher for someone who's been through this. The self-doubt, even a kind of odd shame about their experiences, precludes a kind of easy, relaxed interaction with other people. If you see someone who's interesting, intelligent, open-minded, someone who accepts a wide range of possibility, and yet that person has a lot of trouble, which they shouldn't be having, with relationships and self-esteem and everything else, those are earmarks of having gone through these abduction experiences. I don't want that to sound depressing for people who've been through these experiences. The degree of success of many, many people I've worked with is enormous, yet they don't really believe in it themselves. One person is a nationally known star in the entertainment business; another person is a self-made millionaire from a poverty-stricken background, with a very important place in the real world — yet neither of these people has the self-esteem of Dan Quayle. It's unfortunate. There's an enormous disparity between their actual talents and abilities, their actual accomplishments, and the way they view themselves. And I think that's one of the legacies of these experiences.

ML: I'd like to return to that, but first let's wrap up the hypnosis part of our discussion. You're a successful professional artist. How did you get into hypnosis? Why is it that you took up that practice? And at some point, as I understand it, you turned to other professionals for assistance. Did that have any effect on your work?

BH: Here's the sequence of events. We began to discover some missing-time experiences in the early years of my working with this, in 1976. I had no knowledge of hypnosis, but knowing the patterns of working with other investigators, I went to a psychiatrist friend who, oddly enough, was a collector of my artwork — that's how I know him — and offered to exchange a work of mine for some hours of his doing hypnosis. That's how we began. I was one of the first he hypnotized.

One of the really important ways to learn something about hypnosis is to be hypnotized oneself. One has to go through the process. It's a little like training in psychoanalysis — one has to be analyzed. So I went through hypnosis with two different hypnotists, one a psychiatrist and one a psychologist. I was kind of a control subject in all of this, in the beginning. Then I continued working with a number of other psychiatrists and psychologists from 1976 through 1983, seven years, where I didn't do any hypnosis myself. But I sat through hundreds and hundreds of hours of sessions, seeing the techniques of many different psychiatrists, psychologists and so forth.

Toward the end of 1983, I was pressed because of circumstances to do a couple of sessions myself, because we didn't have anybody available at that moment. The technique is extremely easy. There's no trick to it. You know, high school kids read books on it and hypnotize their sisters, and so forth. It's an easy kind of thing to do. The most important thing, of course, is the insight one has, the sense of support, the emotional rapport, all of the intangibles, which are the harder things to learn. But I started doing it at that point, and then had some of the psychiatrists and psychologists with whom I'd been working sit in on my sessions, to give me some pointers. But I'd been sitting through seven years of hypnosis with all kinds of different people. So, I had more acquaintance with it than, I would say, most people in the country outside the ranks of professional hypnotherapists. And at this point, I've been training mental health people to do hypnosis in these particular cases, and I've developed certain techniques which apply and have been most effective.

The interesting thing is, I'm accused by the skeptics, who never cite any cases whatsoever, of leading the witnesses. What they say is, "He obviously leads the witness, because he gets these accounts." Well, any skeptical hypnotist would get the same accounts. My tapes and transcripts are there for anybody who is well qualified to look into them. There is simply no evidence whatsoever that a person can be led in these cases on any kind of major issue. You can lead a witness easily if the details are trivial. If you're a police hypnotist and you're trying to get a conviction, and you want the witness to say that they think it was a gray car rather than a blue car, through a lot of ingratiation and so forth I'm sure you can get the person to change his description of what color the car was. At least certain people you can, because it's not an emotionally loaded issue to that person, it's just a detail. You know, a courtroom lawyer can talk somebody into changing his view of what color the car was too, by a kind of artful series of questions. But in the UFO situation, the person has gone through an extremely strange, extremely traumatic experience, and to get them to say something different about that experience is virtually impossible, because the person has an enormous emotional involvement with these traumatic events. You can't lead people.

ML: There are several kinds of problems that can occur as a result of, or in the context of, hypnosis. One class of problems would be unwanted after-effects, such as depression, even suicidal tendencies. Another kind of problem would be confabulation.[4] What precautions do you take in these areas?

BH: Any kind of investigation you do with anybody on a UFO subject, even if you just sit down and ask the person to tell you what happened, can have as an after-effect supreme depression and confusion. Confabulation, of course, can come along in just a simple conversation, if we're talking about somebody making things up, or having just read something in a book and thinking maybe they've had something happen. You have those problems all the way along with anybody that you're even just talking to.

Now, hypnosis makes those problems greater, because the emotional re-enactment or reliving of the experience can be extremely dramatic. Yet, most of the people who have really looked into this from a mental health point of view feel that there is something cathartic about getting this repressed imagery out on the table, so to speak — living through some of the same trauma that they've been suffering from without knowing why. One psychotherapist used the example of taking a thorn out of the foot. It's painful when it comes out, there's a stirring up of the pain, but once the thorn is out there's a healing process that ensues.

Having worked with people for fifteen years now, I've seen nothing but what I would consider emotional health result from getting these experiences out on the table, switching on the light, getting a look at what it was that happened. One of the things that goes along with it is that you find out what *didn't* happen. It's like finally going to the doctor and finding out that, OK, you've got a bad flu, but you don't have cancer. You find out what the truth is, and the truth can at least settle some of the worries, even though it might be an unpleasant truth. But what you find out didn't happen is extraordinarily important. And since I work closely with mental health people all the time, many of whom are abductees themselves, these people are resources for future therapy for anybody who needs it.

I would never think of proceeding with somebody who I felt was emotionally unstable. To give you an example, because he does state his own emotional instability, the writer Whitley Strieber, when he approached me, talked about having been suicidal. In fact, he's credited me with having saved his life, and inscribed his book to me exactly that way, "You saved my life." But I was quite aware, from the things he was saying about his own emotional instability, that I wasn't going to proceed with working with him. I insisted upon his working with a psychiatrist for therapy and another psychiatrist for hypnotic regression. It just seemed to me irresponsible to work with him myself. I'm not a trained therapist and make no pretense of being.

But very many people have had these experiences that have caused deep psychological scars, yet they're functioning individuals. They have a home and a life, and they're not talking about jumping out the fifth story window, as Strieber said over and over again. So, in many cases, it's a simple kind of therapeutic act to remember what happened, to understand it, to come to terms with it and go on with one's life, instead of having to live a life of terror, all the lights on at night, unable to sleep. At least when you do explore your experiences, you understand the sources of those fears, and those fears tend to diminish immediately.

ML: You've written that there are serious pros and cons to be considered by anybody who wants to explore the possibility that they may be an abductee. What cautions do you convey to these people?

BH: We have a little information pamphlet that deals with this, which we mail out to everybody who requests information about this, simply because we want to alert everybody at the outset that what they're doing is extraordinarily serious. It's a big step. This is not trivial. If somebody just says, well, I'm curious to find out what's going on — curiosity is never enough. Unless I feel that the person is suffering and that this would be therapeutically beneficial, I won't even think of doing hypnosis with them or looking into their experiences.

One of the first things I try to find out is something about that person's actual life and circumstances. Are you married? Are you in a relationship? Whom do you have at home that you could talk to about this? Do you have a kind of built-in safety net, so to speak? I insist that people have others around them who they feel are very supportive of themselves in delving into this. If a person says, well, I'm in the middle of a divorce, I just lost my job — if there's some current event in their life that's very upsetting — I'll say this is not the time to start looking into these experiences. You have to get these other things settled first, come to terms with the more immediate, pressing problems. If you've had UFO experiences — and you may not have, but if you have — you've been living with this all your life. If you're 35 years old, you've been living with it a long time. Straighten out your immediate problems first, and then we can talk about it later.

So there are the cautions: not to look into this, not to add to your burden of worries, if you are at this moment going through a lot of other problems. Obviously, it's very hard to tell whether people are telling you the truth when they answer these questions. One hopes that they are. One gets a sense. Having done this for fifteen years, I don't feel that I've added to the burdens of many people, although it's possible that I have, because one can't be sure all the time. But I certainly know that it's been demonstrably helpful to the vast majority of people to have explored their experiences.

ML: You've recently created the Intruders Foundation. What's that organization doing?

BH: We realized that we needed funding. If somebody writes me a letter — and I've gotten literally thousands upon thousands of letters — and they desperately want somebody to deal with their UFO experiences, I have to read the letter, answer the letter, send out a little information kit, consult the atlas to find out where the person's home town is in relation to where we have the nearest person who could be of help to them, put the stamps on the letter, and so forth. I've been paying for all of this out of my own pocket for years. My wife says that every time I sell a copy of the book, it costs me five dollars. I decided that this is ridiculous. I felt that a non-profit foundation would be a good way to get contributions for the work, so I set up this foundation for that purpose. We have a quarterly newsletter. We have found it more efficient to use this framework for handling the volume of mail and making sure that people are more efficiently contacted by somebody who can be helpful. We want this to be solely focused on the abduction aspect of the UFO phenomenon. It's not an organization like MUFON, which is studying the entire phenomenon. We're taking just the abduction aspect of it, and it's been working very well.

We're doing our first big conference in January, 1991, at Temple University. This will be a closed conference for psychiatrists, mental health people, medical people and UFO investigators, a whole weekend of discussing training, new techniques of working with people, hypnosis, and the latest information about the nature of the phenomenon.[5]

ML: Have you dealt with very many multiple-witness cases and would you agree that such cases are inherently more solid than single-witness cases?

BH: Any case can be looked at in different ways. One is how much information the case contains that's new or important or interesting. Another is how much probative weight it throws into the scales. Of course, a case with physical evidence and multiple witnesses is much more helpful. I pay more attention to those cases.

One of the cases I've been working with involves a family of seven people, all of whom were involved in the same incident. I've interviewed all of them but one, who's since passed away. The corroboration is extremely important, and it's a terrific case.

ML: Has the phenomenon of animal mutilation figured in any of your cases, and if so, how?

BH: I've run into some cases where animal mutilation events seem to have occurred around certain people who were abductees. It's not something I often run into, due I suppose to the sample of people who are contacting me, but I take the animal mutilation problem very seriously. Dr. John Altshuler, who's been working with Linda Howe and others on this, is a marvelous pathologist, and I think his evidence is very persuasive that the cuts are made by some non-earthly technology. I think that the scoop-marks and scars on human bodies, the particular pattern of cuts and the cellular change around the cuts in animals, as well as the crop circles and their patterns, are all in a strange way variants of the same kind of evidence, traces left behind which are pretty hard to explain away.

ML: You've said that many abductees report seeing certain symbols and other typical things inside alien craft, and that you've kept these details secret to help you corroborate other cases. Without giving away the secret, can you describe this? How often do such reports come up?

BH: This is something I've been looking into only since about the mid-1980s. If we're doing hypnotic regression, we ask the person at a certain point to look around the ship and see if they see anything that might suggest a kind of writing, or script. Now, that in itself is a leading question, but that makes no difference, because what you want, if they do see something, is to reproduce it. Of course, if what they produce is without any kind of connection to the patterns, then it doesn't mean anything. Essentially, I've never gotten people who said yes, they do see something, and then reported or drew something that's not connected at all. Either they say they don't see anything, or they say they do see some kind of writing, in which case, when they reproduce it, it fits the patterns that we get. The patterns are extraordinarily close.

One very important thing to remember about all of this: the people to whom these experiences happen are very ambivalent about what it would mean if this is true. Essentially, they don't want it to be true that they've had these experiences. And so, though one might suppose some sort of elation would come from corroboration of their stories, generally the opposite occurs. It's depressing and frightening when corroboration occurs.

One young woman made a drawing for me of symbols that she saw inside a craft. It was a whole group of them, arranged in an interesting way. Her drawing was virtually identical to the drawings of maybe twenty other abductees. I've worked with this woman a long time and know her well, so, when we finished the session, I just decided to take a chance. I said, "I want to show you what somebody else came up with." I went over and picked up a drawing of virtually identical symbols that had come from another case, and showed them to her. Her reaction was to burst into tears. It wasn't anything like, "Aha, you see, I really did have this." It's more like, "Oh, my God, this did happen to me."

Corroboration, or what the person perceives as corroboration, is generally a depressing fact, rather than something that makes them feel good. So, I've kept this material very secret. It's the kind of thing that you look at and would have to say one of two things: either this absolutely establishes that these people have seen the same kind of craft, literally as they describe; or, a skeptic could only say that I have faked the whole thing and have given these people these things. There's no in-between here. It's either-or, in this case, because there's no other way out.

There are other aspects of abductions which also establish patterns. For example, in our culture, every little child goes in for a physical exam and remembers the doctor pulling out a stethoscope and listening to their heart. As you grow up, you get EKGs, you diet and you worry about your cardio-vascular system. The heart is regarded as *the* organ that we know everything about. It's central to our feelings about health. We know more names of operations having to do with the heart than any other organ. And yet, in not a single solitary abduction case that I have ever heard of, has anybody ever mentioned any alien interest in, or examination of, the human heart. It is simply left out altogether, in all the accounts. People will describe all kinds of things that occur to the reproductive system, the lower abdomen, the head, nose, eyes and ears, even sometimes the feet. But nobody ever mentions the human heart. Now obviously, again, if this were fantasy of some sort, if these stories are bubbling out of people's dream world, knowing our concern with the human heart, we would have to have thousands of stories of an alien interest in the human heart, by the natural random play of fantasy and imagination. But, in fact, we don't have a single one. Which, very much like the symbols, has to tell you something: that there is a precise, hard-edged pattern here which has nothing to do with human fantasy or imagination.

ML: What sense do you have of possible government interest in the abduction phenomenon, and have you personally had any contact with government agencies?

BH: I never have that I know of, although God knows they may be listening to what we're saying at this very moment. My basic point here is that I stay out of government cover-up issues. That's partly because all of those cases are two cans of worms instead of one. I always say, don't believe a single thing either an alien or a government agent tells you about this phenomenon, so I stay out of the double-whammy where the two problems are superimposed. What I'm also trying to do is to make public everything I have. I don't have a lot of secrets. The names and addresses of the abductees, plus these few things that I hold back, are my whole big box of secrets. Everything else I publish. So, I don't know that a government agent would find out much from me that they wouldn't know otherwise.

I think the reason that I haven't been harrassed is that what I'm doing isn't causing the government any trouble. If anything, I'm cleaning up their messes for them. I think the government is loaded to the gills with its own abduction cases, involving probably members of the Joint Chiefs of Staff on down and on up, so if I'm working with a dentist from New Jersey or a housewife from Indiana, I don't think the government is particularly interested in that. This phenomenon is so vast — it isn't that I have any privileged information. There's so much information to be had because this has happened to so many people; it's a pervasive thing. So I don't feel threatened by either the aliens or the government. As I say, I publish my secrets, and there's nothing I want more than to bring this whole subject before a large number of people every time I talk about it.

ML: You've mentioned several times that the abduction phenomenon is vast, so let's talk numbers. How widespread do you think it is, and where do your figures come from?

BH: That's one more thing that I don't want to get into, because it would sound too crazy. But we have done some tests. David Jacobs[6] has developed a questionnaire that he uses with his students at Temple University, which contains subtle questions suggesting UFO experiences. The outcome of those tests would imply that a lot of people — let's put it that way — have had these experiences. I have identified perhaps fourteen or fifteen people who have turned out to be abductees who were personal friends or business acquaintances of mine for years before the UFO subject even came up. To find fourteen or fifteen who are abductees from just that circle of people has to tell me something. I've done enough talk shows and interviews to have discovered that the number of people out there who respond legitimately, in my opinion, and even people who are in the media who have had these experiences, is staggering. It just seems impossible to me that this hasn't involved an enormous number of people. Now, that doesn't make any sense, but it happens to be true. A lot of the data doesn't make sense from a human perspective, but we're not working with a human perspective. It certainly doesn't make sense from a "CIA" perspective, to be running around, starting in 1929, putting implants in people's heads. The numbers are vast.

ML: Were you ever concerned that going public with your findings could result in contaminating your future research, and have you had any second thoughts about that since you did go public?

BH: I've had to give thought to all of these issues. It's an ongoing process of weighing the pros and cons, as to what you make public. Obviously, I have weighed making public my idea of numbers and decided not to go into it. I still try to be careful about all this. But I get letters, for instance, from people who say, "Even if I don't hear from you, even if you don't read this letter, it has helped me enormously to have sat down and written it." And I have no doubt at all that there are a number of people alive today who would not be living if those books hadn't been written. They would have been driven to suicide just by the sense of hopelessness and confusion and self-doubt and terror that they're living with — post-traumatic stress disorder in some cases. Just to have been able to provide a safety valve for such people, so that they feel, "Thank God I'm not crazy, thank God I'm not alone," that is enough, in terms of saving lives, to have justified the entire enterprise.

I've looked into cases where suicide attempts have been made by teenagers prior to the parent getting hold of my book, and then the parent realizes that this child is talking about terrifying figures with huge eyes coming in at night and doing things to the child, and there are physical marks and so forth. The parent is then able to talk to the child, and the child is able to hear a little bit about what has happened to other children. Putting people together so that they're able to have someone to commiserate with and understand their plight has been an enormously therapeutic effort for society as a whole. So I really haven't any regrets about anything I've written.

ML: Some researchers speculate that the abduction phenomenon is specifically related to an alien-human hybridization program. What evidence do you have on this possiblity of hybridization?

BH: In essence, I believe I'm the one who dropped this theory onto the world's table, with *Intruders*,[7] when I first dealt with the genetic focus of the whole UFO phenomenon.

At an earlier stage of ufology, we mainly used to collect UFO sightings and compare notes on craft. In those days, when we didn't even accept, as David Jacobs has said, that a UFO might have an inside, let alone people in there who are doing something, we were in the position of trying to get the license plate number on the getaway car without having figured out what the crime was. It was a very odd way of proceeding, though maybe the only way we could have at the time. I think by the early 1980s, when the abduction phenomenon became more widely seen, we began to understand that the reason they're up there flying around has to do with an interest they have in human beings. They're not here looking for tungsten or something; they're here because they're interested in us.

When I reluctantly came to take seriously the evidence I was getting, it became very clear to me that the whole purpose behind the UFO phenomenon from the beginning has been this reproductive focus — that they are here because we possess certain physical, genetic, and perhaps emotional or even spiritual things that they desperately need. I feel that they need something desperately that they can only get from us, whatever that may be, and that the hybridization attempts are certainly central to it.

As to whether or not there are people walking around on earth who are hybrids, let me put it this way. With all the difficulties we have between parents and children, just the normal, good old-fashioned human psychological problems and difficulties, supposing you throw into that hopper the idea that a parent has a child in the house who maybe isn't 100 percent theirs, or 100 percent human. Just supposing that idea was dropped in: the chaos and paranoia that would add to the normal mix of life's problems is a risk I don't want to run. So I don't like to get into that issue, because I can see only trouble resulting from it. Let's just say it's a theory we'll leave out on the table, and whoever wants to kick it around can. But I don't think it's helpful. Life is tough enough without it.

ML: Would you be willing to explain what led you to think that hybridization is really what's going on?

BH: I took a whole book to do that, in *Intruders*. Here, let me just cite a recent case. A woman finds herself waking up at five in the morning in her four-year-old son's bed, after she had just been staring out the window at a moving light that was shining a beam down on the ground. Soon after, this woman became pregnant and assumed that it was a natural kind of pregnancy, and she was very pleased to have another child. She went to the gynecologist, got a positive blood and urinalysis test, got ultrasound, a little fetus was found with a heartbeat and so forth. Three months into the pregnancy, she had some strange feelings and spotting, and she felt something was the matter. She went back to her gynecologist. They checked into it with ultrasound and found that the fetus had no heartbeat and was a little smaller than it should be at three months. Because her husband is a doctor connected with the same hospital and they were giving her class-A care, she was immediately sent up-stairs to a neo-natalogist, who did another sonogram, found no heartbeat and said, "No doubt about it, this is not a living fetus. It's going to have to be removed." So she came back about five hours later for the D&C. Meanwhile, something extremely unusual had happened which suggests an abduction. But she came in for the D&C, and they did it. They found an umbilical cord, the placenta and so forth, but there was no fetal tissue whatsoever. They had intended to check whether there was some genetic or other problem with the fetus, so the remains were to be sent to the pathology lab. This is routinely done. But there were no remains. So, within a period of about five hours, two different people saw the fetus on ultrasound, and then it disappeared.

I have another case that I'm just beginning to look into, where a woman went to bed five and a half months pregnant and woke up with no fetus, a flat belly and no sign of discharge of any sort, having also had the experience of paralysis and her room filling up with light in the middle of the night.

Some cases include descriptions of the hybrid children. I have a wonderful description of hybrid children from two normal human children who have been picked up and asked to play and interact with hybrid children. One of these human children is four and a half years old, and the other is six. They described the hybrid children the same way they're described in other cases, as having large heads and white hair which is very sparse and patchy. And this poor little boy said, "I don't want this to happen any more. I don't like them. I'm afraid of them. They don't understand my games, and I don't understand their games." It's as if there's an attempt to have an interaction develop between these hybrid children from an obviously alien culture, and our own children. The evidence is piling up on every front that this is going on, and this seems to be what the whole UFO phenomenon is about.

ML: In the recent book, *Gods of Eden*,[8] author William Bramley makes a case that aliens have manipulated human development for a very long time. Along a similar line, Bob Lazar states that during his time at S 4, he was shown a book that had signs of being of alien manufacture, in which the writer said that aliens had "externally corrected" the evolution of human beings many dozens of times. Such ideas prompt speculation in a somewhat different direction than you've taken. Is this program of alien activity an act of desperation, or is it a science project?

BH: I've met Bob Lazar and he seems like a very nice man, although I've never had the chance to talk to him. But it seems he's been presented with a document which is either of government origin, alien origin, or perhaps a collaboration. I've said that those are the two sources not to take seriously — or one does so at one's own risk, though they might be telling the truth from time to time. So we have a problem here.

As far as trying to decide whether there's been alien manipulation for a long time, that's highly speculative. There's no way of knowing. I'm very much a pragmatist, so I deal with what I can actually find out in a direct way. I've been struck by what seems to me to be an increasing number of cases that are more overt, less covert abductions, and which would suggest a kind of desperation. What's causing that I don't really know, but I suspect that these events are incredibly more dense now than they ever were in any period in history before. Whether or not we've had abductions before my 1929 record of early ones, I don't know. I think if they were common before, we would have gotten more odd stories, the kinds of things that would suggest possible abductions. These stories do exist, but they're not very common. On the other hand, the problems I'm seeing right now are so enormous, the pain and human suffering are so great, and the momentum of the abduction phenomenon is so great, that it seems to be an example more of desperation and emergency rather than cool scientific detachment. I may be completely wrong on that, but that's my gut feeling.

ML: In the introduction to your book *Intruders*, you point out that people find some ideas to be inherently unbelievable despite massive evidence. Do you think the general public still finds the prospect of an alien presence here basically unbelievable, or do you see a change?

BH: I think it's changed enormously. I've been struck by recent comments on public political polling, that polsters have been always amazed, and they certainly shouldn't be, that they've gotten misleading results so many times because people find it embarrassing to state their true position on certain issues. We've found, for example, that polsters very much underestimated the degree of racist feeling in various contests where you had a black challenger and a white incumbent. More people felt inclined to say that they supported the black man than in fact happened in the election. The hidden racist factor might be as much as ten percent. Now, what that means is, people understand with a poll, in certain cases, there's a respectable side and an unrespectable side. Concerning UFOs, when people were asked in a poll, "What do you think other people think of UFOs?," the vast majority thought that other people didn't think UFOs were a legitimate subject. This is interesting. It shows the social perspective that it's a negative to say you accept this. Still, within that context, a majority in the last Gallup poll, however you split up the undecideds, said that they believe UFOs are physically real, rather than imaginary. Therefore, I think a large majority of the public actually believes UFOs are physically real.

I think that the cumulative effect of all of us in this field who have done any kind of public education on the subject has been positive. With *Intruders* a best seller, I was treated extremely fairly by major interviewers on the Today Show, and 20/20, the Canadian Broadcasting Company, BBC, National Public Radio and so forth. The people who have interviewed me have been respectful and serious about it. The New York Times, Washington Post and other respectable papers have reviewed the book favorably. That has to have an effect on public opinion. And now my book has appeared in a British edition, as well Dutch, Italian and Spanish editions, and is due out shortly in Japanese. It's going to be appearing in Polish, German, Portuguese and Swedish. The Russians are interested in it. The number of places in which this is being taken seriously is, I would say, astonishing compared to the way the subject was looked at fifteen or twenty years ago.

ML: Along with the able and frequently courageous work of independent researchers in changing public opinion, it's been acknowledged by some of those same researchers that there seems to be a shift in the government cover-up. Do you think that's occurring? What do you see?

BH: I think what you mean is that some people feel there's a deliberate easing of the government cover-up in preparation for...whatever. I don't know that I've seen that happen. A basic rule of government intelligence is, if you have a huge secret that has to involve thousands of people, and the secret really can't be kept with such a huge number of people, the most immediate way of cutting the damage is to surround the truth with disinformation. For instance, D-Day involved hundreds of thousands of people. The secret had to be widely known as to where we were going to land, but they managed to confuse the Germans with numerous other versions of where we were going to land. I think government disinformation has been the basic tool of keeping this secret, and I think the disinformation efforts are just as strong now as they ever were, maybe even stronger.

When the government cover-up issue was aired on the television program "UFO Cover-up: Live," one of the things that came out was that our so-called "captive aliens" sit around listening to Haydn and eating strawberry ice cream, and also they created Jesus Christ. I could almost see a room where a bunch of government people are saying, "What would lose the most credibility for this subject? What can we say that would make it seem totally ridiculous?" Of course, all disinformation has to contain truthfulness. So what you do is, you release or suggest anatomical information about aliens which seems truthful, and then you wed it to the idea that they really love strawberry ice cream and sit around listening to Haydn. What you hope is that the whole thing goes down the tube together, like trying to mislead the D-Day landing. So, since I see no lessening of government disinformation, I don't see that the government is getting ready to let us know anything about it.

The fact is that the information simply can't be kept under wraps anymore. It's just bursting out at the seams. And I think our little friends from the sky, whoever they are, are aiding and abetting this slow consciousness-raising that's taking place for the public to accept that these things are real. When I was in England recently, I was on a program speaking about abductions, and another man spoke about crop circles, saying that this was a natural phenomenon, that there were whirlwinds and so forth. The very next day, I was interviewed by a couple of BBC people, and they brought me a photograph from the morning paper which showed a new crop circle configuration, two very complex circles inside circles, connected by a long channel, like a barbell. But arranged across it, at regular intervals, were gigantic rectangles, which were probably some thirty feet by eight feet and just placed absolutely regularly in a row, symmetrically across this basic barbell configuration. It's almost as if somebody flying around up there said, "OK, so you say they're whirl-winds? We'll give you rectangles. Let's see what you do with that one."[9] It's almost as if there's a countering on their part, perhaps not deliberately, but perhaps deliberately — who knows? — of some of the disinformation and debunking that's going on.

I feel that we have much more evidence on all of this now than we had even two years ago. The evidence is just coming out of the closet left and right. I don't think the government is releasing that information. I think the government simply can't control it. The government — whatever we mean when we say "the government" — is like the little Dutch boy who's stuck, because all his toes and fingers are stuck in the dike and he can't even move, but the leaks are occurring down the row a bit. I think the government is helpless. I don't think the government is initiating this.

There may be people on the inside who want this to be made public. But frankly, what can the government gain by making public a situation in which they would have to say, "OK gang, this is really going on. They're flying around, and there isn't anything we can do about it. They can take whomever they wish, whenever they wish, do whatever they wish and bring them back, and we haven't got a single defense. There's no sign that they're ultimately going to be friendly, although so far they haven't been malevolent." That's the government announcement. How could the government make such a confession of complete impotence? It's like a hospital saying, "OK, we're going to close up. There's nothing we can do about disease anymore." It's an impossible thing. You would have, I think, national panic. I think many people can entertain the idea of UFOs flying around, but the idea that they may be here doing things, taking our kids for medical experiments and bringing them back at will — and that this is extremely widespread — I think this would cause panic.

ML: In a pamphlet for the Intruders Foundation, you've written that it's very important to remain open to what you called "the broadening value" of the UFO experience. You yourself have been exposed to mind-boggling things. How has this broadened you, and how have you coped with it?

BH: I think that if I've coped successfully, and I don't know that I have, it's by keeping my focus of attention on the people who have had these experiences and what it's meant to them, and by trying to get them on an even keel as best I can, bringing them together with one another and so forth. In other words, by building a sense of solidarity with my fellow humans. That, I think, is the strongest thing. If you begin to focus on whomever it is flying around up there, and sit around wondering whether they're time travelers or meta-terrestrials or whatever — all that, I think, is somehow counter-productive. It only leaves you lost and wondering.

This is where we live, and our fellow humans are the main action. So, I think that keeping as grounded as possible, and trying to keep the other people as grounded as possible, is the best way to cope with this.

In terms of broadening, my role as an artist has to do with raising questions in my work that have to do with all the ultimate issues. As Gauguin said, "Who are we, where do we come from, where are we going?" That's the title of one of his paintings. I think of the role of the artist as a kind of mediator, rather than a priest; he's the mediator between the questions and the problems, the physical material and all of those ultimate questions. I think that art has always been meant to provide a kind of solace and a way of giving specific expression to whatever those ultimate doubts and curiosities and worries and obsessions are. We all face death, and we all wonder, as Gauguin did, why we're here in the first place. I suppose I can address those questions in my work, which is really wonderful.

I can imagine that if I were selling aluminum siding and trying to do this same kind of UFO work, I might have more of a conflicted and hopeless life. But in this case, I think things have worked out. Having a very supportive wife and daughter has been very helpful, too. This is not easy work to do. One of the reasons that I have boxes of unopened letters at home is simply because the amount of pain contained in those letters is something you have to dole out to yourself in slow, even doses. These are people begging for help, very confused, very frightened, filled with self-doubt. You immediately want to pick up the phone and call each one and say, "Calm down, it's OK, you're not crazy. People survive these things. Help is on the way." But of course, if you get thousands and thousands of these letters, it's physically impossible to do it. Again, the reason for the foundation. But just on a personal level, it grinds you down. I get to feel what it must be like for a doctor in an inner-city hospital, who only sees, for example, malformed children, easily preventable disease and so forth, day in and day out. Seeing the heavy, disturbing personal problems that these experiences engender, seeing them come through one after another in totally predictable ways and realizing that you're a grain of sand in the effort that needs to be made to help, can be very depressing. So, thank God there's life and love and sex and music and art and humor, which helps enormously to keep one on an even keel. It's not easy.

ML: In your 1987 article, "What They're Doing to Us,"[10] you suggest that the aliens inflict traumatic experiences on abductees out of ignorance of human psychology rather than malice. Does that explanation still work for you? And how does it relate to the suggestion of Linda Howe and others that the little gray beings usually associated with abduction are perhaps not fully conscious, but may actually be some kind of biological robot?

BH: It's really basic. People feel they're dealing with an alien "something." You can turn to somebody sitting next to you in a bar and strike up a conversation, but there is no way that anybody in these experiences feels they're dealing with that kind of equivalence to themselves. So, whether the thing is a robot or whatever, it's alien, and it's felt as alien. Calling it a non-living whatever doesn't really help, because it doesn't clarify anything. The point is that the alien nature of this means they simply are not like us.

We get through life partly by the fact that we can read another's face, we can read their body language, we can get some sense of emotion. All of those things are denied us during contact with aliens. There's really no way we can tell what they understand about us. Their understanding might be incredibly subtle in some ways, but miss on some other major things. There's no way to know.

But I don't see signs of deliberate malice. One man I've worked with who is an abductee said to me, "Budd, when I was standing there with them, if I could have thought of them as enemies and cranked myself up with hate, I would have somehow handled the whole thing better. But," he said, "it was the ambivalence of not knowing what this is, the total confusion. This isn't an enemy, it isn't a friend, it's not like me. What is it? I can't read it." He said the confusion added to his sense of helplessness.

I think we have this tremendous human need to put black hats or white hats on everybody. You know, thank God somebody like Saddam Hussein comes along and acts it out for us, so we can say, "Boy, there's a villain for you." We need that. But we can't do that at all with the UFO thing. We have never gotten a savior out of this, and we have never gotten a Saddam Hussein out of it either. The fact that they are so different from us has a very subversive effect on our ability to handle this.

ML: If what you're saying is true, then we're dealing with an absolutely profound influence on human history. Where is this leading us?

BH: Again, and this has to do with the way I cope, I try not to ask myself that question. To make a grim analogy, if the future tends in ways that are truly disturbing, which it may, I would rather see myself as the guy on the deck of the Titanic trying to get passengers into the lifeboats and trying to keep a few kids from crying, than worrying about how long the ship's going to stay afloat. If you look at it another way, there are other scenarios. They could leave. They could just get what they need and split, and leave us alone. There could be a well-intended attempt to intermingle, which might have drastic consequences for society. It could all be very benign, although I haven't seen any signs of that.

There could be some ultimate gain, to put the most hopeful light on it. There could be sharing of technology which would get us out of our energy crunch, and a thousand other things. There's really no way to guess. I sympathize with people like Leo Sprinkle[11] who try to put the data into an optimistic framework, to create a scenario that's going to have a happy ending. It would be awfully nice if that were the case. I don't sympathize with the prophets of doom, who seem intent on telling everybody to stock up on food and put an automatic rifle under the bed. I think this is extremely dangerous to do. In the meantime, since we have no sign of anything deliberately malevolent, why stroke all the paranoid tissue and nerves that we all live with too much anyway? I don't know what the end result is going to be. All I can see is that the temporary costs and side-effects are enormous and unfortunate.

In any case, the problem needs addressing. As I always say, an extraordinary phenomenon demands an extraordinary investigation. After our long conversation here, anybody reading this who feels they can sit on the sidelines and wait for something to happen is abdicating responsibility.

Chapter Five
Tom: Personal Encounters

"Tom" is a long-time resident of Santa Barbara, California, who claims to have experienced many UFO-related events through-out his adult life, as well as strange childhood encounters that suggest alien contact. Because he believes that open discussion of these events might jeopardize his reputation and also cause discomfort to several people who have experienced events with him, he has asked that his real name not be used here.

Tom contacted me by phone in the summer of 1990 after reading the first publication of the 2020 Group Visitors Investigation Project. He told me that he wanted to discuss his experiences with someone who might be able to make use of them for research and educational purposes. I met him face to face a short time later and quickly recognized that his story contains many elements of a classic multiple-abduction case. It is presented here as one person's testimony to the mystery and intricacy of human-alien encounter.

Most of the details in this narrative have been recalled without the aid of hypnosis. Tom suspects that many addi-tional details might be revealed through hypnosis, but as of this writing he says he's not entirely convinced that he's been abducted. He is sure, however, that his UFO encounters have greatly influenced the course of his life. Moreover, unlike many people who regard such encounters as traumatic, Tom takes a positive attitude toward his strange experiences.

Tom's case is inherently strong in the sense that there are additional witnesses to nearly every event he describes. Among these witnesses, I have spoken with Tom's older brother, who lives on the East Coast, and with a long-time acquaintance in Santa Barbara, both of whom corroborated certain aspects of this narrative. I anticipate further investigation of Tom's case in the future. — ML

Michael Lindemann: Describe the first time you saw a UFO.

Tom: That was probably in June of 1971. It involved the sighting of, I believe, three UFOs that were out over the Santa Barbara Channel.[1] They had extremely bright lights that were shining down on the ocean, the brightest lights I've ever seen. They operated in an erratic manner. They'd stay motionless over an area with the light shining down, and then all of a sudden they would go to another area and the light would shine down again. It was about dusk when we saw these — my ex-wife and I were both present at the time — and they appeared for about 20 minutes and then left. When they left, they went straight up at a speed that was beyond my comprehension. I'd never seen anything move that fast. It was like a streak of light just going almost straight up, and they were totally gone.

ML: You said you believe there were three UFOs. Aren't you sure?

T: At first I saw one object, and then there were three objects. I think the two additional objects may have come from the one original object, or they may have just appeared. I was so transfixed on the event that I think I was looking at one object and then suddenly realized that there were others. I'm not sure how the other two arrived. Suddenly they were just there.

ML: Did all three look the same?

T: They appeared to be similar in size. From my vantage point, they looked huge. With the Channel Islands and the coastline as a reference, I'd say they were probably the size of a football field. I'm not sure if all three went behind the islands, or just one or two of them, but I could see the islands back-lit by these extremely bright lights. I don't know of anything that could back-light the islands — not anything we know about, that's for sure. It was very difficult to believe.

ML: When the sighting ended, did you see one object go straight up, or more?

T: They were separated by some distance, and my perception is that they all went straight up, at a slight angle. They went up so fast that I couldn't follow them. They were there one minute, and then they were gone.

There were a number of other witnesses to this sighting who were friends of ours. I hadn't known they were there until we talked with them later. It was a rather interesting sighting, because I didn't really believe in UFOs at the time, and I didn't really know what I had seen. I thought it might be some kind of Air Force craft or something like that. But their movements just defied gravity, as far as I was concerned. They would stop and go on a dime, and make right-angle turns that would probably have killed or seriously injured anybody inside. So, they were not conventional aircraft.

ML: It sounds as if this sighting predated your academic interest in the subject of UFOs.

T: Yes. I really had no interest in UFOs at that time. But I couldn't believe the experiences that followed in the next four years, just one right after another.

ML: Would you like to describe a few experiences from that period that stand out in your mind?

T: The next significant encounter was in August of 1971, in eastern Canada around the Great Lakes. At the time, my wife and I didn't know it was a UFO. We just figured it was something really strange.

We were driving across Canada at night, and my wife had stopped to get coffee at a truck stop. I remember she came out very distraught, because it turned out to be a whorehouse for truckers. She got her coffee and continued driving. I had been driving all day, so I was asleep in the front seat of the truck —

we had a small pickup truck and camper. The next thing I remember is that I woke up, and there was this bright light behind us, just one light. I looked back and couldn't see headlights. I just saw this mass of light behind us. It was so bright that our headlights didn't even look like they were on. My wife was waiting for this thing to pass. She thought it was a truck or something, and it hadn't passed, so she finally decided to start accelerating our truck. I looked over at the speedometer, and it was close to 100 miles an hour. This thing was right on our tail. I couldn't believe that a truck, especially a big semi or something, could be doing that kind of speed, because they're just not geared for that. Then, like almost instantly, the next thing I remember is that we were by the side of the road, it was pitch black, and there were no lights around anywhere.

We had no idea if there was missing time involved in that. It wasn't until I saw the movie *Close Encounters of the Third Kind*, actually a number of times, that I realized this incident was similar to something depicted in that movie. We didn't talk much about it afterward. My wife and I talked about it briefly, and then we decided it was just not an incident that needed to be brought up again, so we didn't bring it up — which I thought was very strange, because it was a very significant incident. In essence, we were being chased by a huge light down this road. I have a very vivid memory of that incident, and for some reason, we weren't supposed to talk about it. And that's one of the significant things that I remember about a lot of these events, that I just felt I wasn't supposed to talk about them.

ML: You were racing down the road at 100 miles an hour with the light right on your tail, and suddenly you were at the side of the road, stopped, pitch dark, lights gone — and you don't know how that happened. Is that correct?

T: Yes, that's correct. I don't have a clear time reference for the overall sequence of events, because I had been asleep and woke up just as this incident started to occur. I do know that the time from 100 miles an hour to dead-stopped at the side of the road was almost instantaneous.

ML: From the sound of it, this is the kind of discontinuity that one might associate with an abduction experience. What's your feeling about being abducted? Do you consciously recollect or believe you have been abducted?

T: I believe I may have been, but I don't consciously recall actual physical abduction. The problem is that I have read extensively about UFOs and abduction experiences, so I try not to mix this acquired knowledge of the subject into my own personal thing. I'm extremely careful about what I say in that respect. I do feel that I've had a number of experiences that have the classic symptoms of an abduction. However, I can't tell you for sure that that's what occurred.

ML: You said that you felt after your experience with the light that it was something you shouldn't talk about. What's that feeling about? Why do you think you felt that way?

T: That feeling has been prevalent throughout my experiences. In many cases, I thought people would just think I was crazy, so I didn't choose to discuss it very much except within a circle of friends who might understand what I was talking about.

In November of 1990, Budd Hopkins did a hypnotic regression on me, and we looked into an incident that occurred in 1975, where I actually saw a UFO on the ground and walked under and around it. Prior to this regression, I always thought that I didn't want to touch the object. But what happened in the regression was that as I walked up to the object, I had a tingling sensation all over my body, and my right kneecap and my right wrist started aching. I started to touch the object on the ground, and I was told not to touch it. As I reached toward it, I could feel a strange tingling sensation in my fingers and my hand. I've never felt anything quite like that. It was like somebody said to me, "Don't touch it." So I didn't touch the object. But I didn't remember, until we got into the hypnotic regression, that there was actually a voice in my head that was saying, "Don't touch it."

ML: Let's reconstruct this incident from the beginning.

T: It was in September or October of 1975. I was coming back from having dinner in Buellton, and I decided to drive back along Camino Cielo, which is the road that runs across the top of the mountains in Santa Barbara. As I was traveling east on Camino Cielo, near the intersection of Painted Cave Road, my lights caught something that was off on a fire-break road as I made a turn. It was probably 9:30 or 10:00 in the evening.

I decided to drive up the fire-break road to see what was there, and what I found was a giant object that had three legs sticking out of it. My immediate thought was that it was a fire tower, because throughout the mountains up there they have large concrete structures that collect water for use in fighting fires. I thought this was a new type of structure. But on closer examination, it was an object that was made of a material that I had never encountered before. It didn't have any seams or rivets. I drove up to the object and got out of the car. I walked around and underneath the object. Basically, it was saucer-shaped, probably 35 to 40 feet in diameter. It stood about six or seven feet off the ground, with three legs extended to keep it perfectly level. There were no markings of any kind on it.

I parked my car just a little way away from it and allowed the lights to shine underneath it. I could not see the top very easily, but it looked to be about fifteen feet high. The material kind of looked like one piece, as if it were made in a mold or something. It was sort of a dull silvery-gray color, but it did not appear to be metal. I don't know what it was. At the time, there was no noise, no lights, no sign of any activity whatsoever.

There was a girl with me, with whom I'd gone out to dinner, and she was kind of freaking out and wanted to leave, so we did. I remembered in the hypnotic regression that I had a tingling sensation when I was around the vehicle. When I left, the tingling sensation almost completely subsided.

I drove a very short distance back to the main road and encountered what looked to be a rock on the road. It turned out to be an owl that all of a sudden flew straight at my windshield and over the car. This is a situation that had happened to me dozens of times in that area. And that was the point where there was missing time. From that particular moment in my trip, there's three or four miles that I couldn't account for. I couldn't account for driving it at all, although I know I had to have driven it. But the next recollection I have is of driving down the pass [having gotten to Highway 154 from Camino Cielo], and arriving in Santa Barbara probably an hour or more later than I thought it was supposed to be.

The fact that owls seem to have been a common occurrence when I've had a segment of missing time or a UFO sighting is something I never believed to have any significance until I got into researching and found that owls are one of the things that may be involved in screen memories. There were numerous times over the years that I had been on that same stretch of road and had seen an owl suddenly fly at me. Quite often I would find myself three, four or five miles away from where I thought I was as a result. I would not remember driving the distance. And this used to concern me a lot. I thought that there was something wrong, but I always charged it off that the owl had distracted me and I didn't realize where I was.

ML: How often would you say you've experienced missing time in encounters of this sort?

T: I've documented missing time on at least 22 occasions where there were UFO sightings or related activities. Many of them were centered around the sighting of an owl, many of them when driving in that same particular area.

ML: Did you go back and try to verify that the physical thing was actually there?

T: I was very curious about it. The next day, I went back to see if it was still there, thinking that it might possibly have been a water tank that the forest service had brought in. It was gone, and I looked for evidence that it had been there. The ground up there was very hard-packed. It's sort of decomposed rock, with a very granular surface. The wind had been blowing hard that evening, probably 20 to 30 miles an hour. There was no evidence that it had been there.

ML: Your friend, the woman who was with you, evidently also saw this. Did you discuss it afterwards?

T: We discussed it very briefly, as to "What the heck was that?" Basically, she became very jumpy and wanted to leave the area as quickly as possible. She did not get out of the car. She didn't want to talk about it later, and she never went out with me again. I think that the incident probably was very upsetting to her, and I don't think she wanted to be around anybody who had incidents like this happening. Her name was Irene, and I've lost track of her over the years.

ML: I'd like to backtrack a bit. We've been talking mostly about incidents that occurred in the 1970s. Are there incidents in your earlier life that seem to be related? How far back do these go?

T: They go back to about 1950. I was three years old at that time, and I would never have dreamt that they had anything to do with UFOs, except that my brother brought the incidents up because he was very irritated about what had occurred.

During my early childhood, I had an imaginary friend. I think that many children may go through this, where they have an imaginary friend. I always called him my Whodie. My Whodie was a little different from most imaginary friends in the sense that things happened: objects were moved, things got broken and other things occurred that a three-year-old wasn't capable of doing. My brother used to get blamed for all of these things, and quite often he was severely punished for these things that my Whodie did. My parents thought that I was making up this creature, but I was convinced I was not. My Whodie was very real to me. I also have unclear memories of being examined and controlled by strange people who were my size.

These experiences occurred from 1950 until about 1957, and then they stopped. I don't know what they were. I can only say that they might have been UFO-related.

ML: Can you recall any particular instance of a thing getting moved or broken?

T: I can't tell you anything specific. All I remember now is that there was a big family controversy over my Whodie [see Briefing]. My brother is the one who reminded me, because I had completely forgotten about it. There were a lot of things that happened that I wasn't capable of, so my brother got blamed for them.

At that time, my family lived in a heavily wooded area of Connecticut, right on Long Island Sound. There were swamps and marshland all around there, with large boulders, little ponds and that sort of thing. I spent a lot of time wandering around in the woods

continued page 178

BRIEFING

Other Tales of the "Imaginary Friend"

The being that Tom calls his Whodie might be the product of a child's imagination. But it might be something more. To find out how Tom's family felt about the Whodie, I spoke with his older brother, who lives in an eastern state. Like Tom, he wishes to remain anonymous. Here, I'll call him Bill.

Bill said the Whodie played a big role in his family, primarily as the subject of jokes. He confirmed that there were many occasions when Tom blamed the Whodie for losing or breaking small items around the house, or for other forms of mischief. Usually, these claims were treated lightly. Years after Tom and Bill left home, their father would still mockingly blame the Whodie if something turned up missing. But their father was also a strict disciplinarian, and sometimes "he got fed up with this imaginary person," Bill says. On more than one occasion, Tom took a beating for some mischief he said was the Whodie's doing; but he never changed his story. In Bill's words, "We all thought it was an excuse he was using. But Tom was dead serious."

continued next page

Briefing, continued

Bill won't say whether or not the Whodie was real, much less an alien being. But he doesn't rule out the possibility, because he had an impressive UFO encounter while serving in the military.

In any case, the Whodie remains a decades-old recollection from Tom's childhood. However, adults also report such mischievous beings. In May of 1991, I interviewed a group of men and women ranging in age from 31 to 68, all of whom described recent personal experiences similar to Tom's tale of the Whodie. Here is one of those accounts.

Marty (not his real name) is a 31-year old aerospace worker. He has held a high security clearance and has worked on super-secret "black" projects. As this book goes to press, Tom and Marty have no knowledge of one another. The following words are Marty's:

"I feel that there is an alien presence involved. I've had conscious experiences that relate to that, a sensing of something being there, of being surrounded by something. The key thing is that I have had for seven [years], basically since I've been working on aircraft, the experience of things happening in my home, or around me. I call them my little friends. But they move things, shut doors, open doors. Things that I know I set down somewhere...they're gone, and then they're back. Like, if I put my keys on the table, and the next morning I went to find my keys, I couldn't find them on the table. Go upstairs, look around, go back down, and they're on the table. Things like that, mischievous things...

"Within the last week, during my absence from home, my wife experienced the movement of things in the house. Books that were on shelves are now sitting on a table. She said that she heard something in the kitchen, got up, and as she entered the kitchen, two of the doors shut. She turned the light on, and the doors shut. She has no explanation for what was going on.

"I call them my little friends simply as a joke, because it can be a frightening experience, not so much for me, but it has been for my wife. You don't enjoy things like this happening.

"Through my experience with aircraft, I've met a lot of military. One thing that I've found in common is that they've experienced a similar thing. In Hawaii, I think the word is mini-huna, the small island gods or whatever. Talking with military personnel who've worked on the smaller islands out there, they said that that type of activity happened every day on the base — things moving, things disappearing, things showing up out of nowhere. They called it the mini-hunas.

"It seems to be a movement of things outside your realm of vision. You know, you catch things moving, and you look, and nothing's moving. Or you hear something move — you hear a door slam — you go and look, and there's no explanation.

"I don't think I've seen my little friends in the conscious state. In the subconscious state, I have. To me, they were more of the demonic type of being. It's hard to discern whether I'm seeing things from Dante's Inferno or envisioning my own image of what a demon would look like. But they seem to be short, thin, with leathery-type skin. It seems that they're never clothed. You don't see any genitals or anything like that, but they're not clothed. The heads are unusually large for the body. At times I've seen horns, or large ears perhaps. The fingers...the image was not of a five-fingered hand, but something different...maybe three fingers, or three fingers and a thumb. Not a normal hand. The feet...toes of an unusual shape, not like a footprint, but wider-based, almost like a suction-cup. For the most part, they had skin with a lizard-type of appearance to it, not scaly, but the kind of color that's common with lizards, kind of a greenish-beige.

"The face is fairly nondescript. The only thing, as far as I can remember, is that the eyes were big and bright. Almost black. The eyes almost had no eyelids, but the eyeball would be almost three times the size of mine.

"They don't seem to have a great deal of what we would call muscular features on their bodies, but they have strength beyond my understanding of muscles. I would say that their muscle structure is completely different than [ours]. They appear to move gracefully and quickly, which would give the indication of...very good muscle capabilities. But they don't appear to have that.

"That's the only [kind of] beings that I've ever experienced or thought that I've experienced. I've never seen them as a physical essence, consciously. The best example, when I saw a great number of them in a dream, was the feeling that I was holding them back from an invasion of earth. I told my wife...I called it 'holding back hell's gates.' The other [way] is basically a subconscious sensing that they were there. The images and dreams that I had, in the vivid sense that I could see them, were from 1985-86. That's when I first started on black projects."

Can any credence be given to images from Marty's dreams? Abduction researchers have come to believe that dream-like recollections often contain important data on alien encounters. Regardless, the odd physical events in Marty's home seem to defy prosaic explanation. Is there some connection between his work in top secret projects and his experience of the "little friends?" Why do so many military people report similar occurrences? Obviously, there is a great deal here that we do not yet understand. — ML when I was young. That's one of the places that the Whodie appeared.

ML: Did you go out there by yourself, or with your friends?

T: I went out there primarily by myself, but the Whodie was quite often there.

ML: Do you mean as a visible, seemingly physical being?

T: That's the way I perceive it, yes. But my recollections are fuzzy, not clear. I was so young at that time that I just don't know how much of it was real, and how much wasn't. It was real to me at the time, I know that.

ML: What did your Whodie look like?

T: The Whodie was a small figure. I remember him being probably three or four feet tall with a large head and large eyes, similar to the classic alien-type person that is often described by abductees.[2] I don't have any clear memory of whether or not he was actually an alien. But that's the feeling I had when I started to go back and really think about it.

ML: Where did the name "Whodie" come from?

T: I recently asked my mother about that, and she has no idea where it came from. Neither do I. It was just a name that was used to describe this entity.

ML: What about your memories of being examined and controlled by strange people who were your size?

T: That occurred in the evening hours in the house where I lived at that time, in rural Connecticut. I recall it happening once, and beyond that I'm not sure. I recall it starting in the second-story bedroom in the back, at the top of the stairs. I was somewhere between three and five years old. I remember the Whodie being there, and that I was not in the bedroom at the time this occurred. I was somewhere else, but I have no idea how I got there. It was a room. I'm trying to be careful here. I have to say it was similar to what I've heard described by abductees, but I hate to say that with any kind of certainty, because I may have been influenced by what I've read. I remember some kind of examination. I remember that the room had lights that seemed to come from everywhere, as if the walls were light. When you're that age, things like this don't bother you. At least, they didn't bother me.

ML: Was your Whodie there?

T: Oh yes.

ML: Do you recall anyone else there besides you and your Whodie?

T: I think there were three, besides my Whodie. I recall that they were similar in size and stature.

ML: Earlier, you used the word "controlled." What does that mean, in this case?

T: On a number of occasions throughout my life, I've felt that my mind was alert but I could not move. I used to attribute these all to dreams, and I was always curious as to why I had them. I've had these so-called dreams where I could not move a muscle, but my mind was very alert. And I would do things like move through walls. I could float, levitate. It's like the spirit leaving the body, where you can go through solid objects. That occurred during my early years and on numerous occasions since. Often in these so-called dreams I would have the experience of falling or rapidly gaining altitude in a horizontal position. I would feel almost completely detached — not physically in control, but mentally in control. One thing I learned about this was that I couldn't move, but I could think of going in another direction and then go in that direction.

ML: What did other entities have to do with that?

T: I don't know, but I think those occurrences may have been at times when I had contact. In almost every case, I had thought that these were dreams, but again, as I started reading accounts of other people going through walls and things like that, I began to realize that this might be what had happened.

Over the years, there have also been many times when an idea will pop into my head that comes from nowhere. This has been significant in the direction that I've taken throughout my life, in the sense that I'll come up with an idea, just out of the blue, that seems to go, seems to work. It's not a verbal communication. It's something that just all of a sudden is there.

ML: Are you saying that some of the ideas that have worked for you are ideas that you have received from other beings? Couldn't you simply attribute these to a good imagination?

T: Well, I'd like to think that everything I've thought of was my idea, but what I'm saying is that sometimes ideas just pop into my head that turn out to be very viable, and I don't know where they came from. That's been a consistent thing throughout my life.

ML: When did your Whodie stop appearing to you?

T: That occurred sometime around 1957, at about age ten. From the time I was six or so, the Whodie appeared less and less frequently. But when I was ten, my family moved from the countryside into town, and my life started to become different. I would say the disappearance of the Whodie coincided with that move.

ML: After your Whodie disappeared, what was your next

experience of an unusual encounter?

T: The next time things started to occur was probably 1970. After going off to college in California, I had gone back to Maryland, where my parents were living at the time and where I had finished high school. There I met a girl who had had a crush on me in high school. We ended up getting married.

The minute I got together with this woman, I started having experiences that went on and on and on. Sometimes we had experiences every month or every few weeks during the time we were together. Many times, we'd just pass them off as imagination or hallucination. We couldn't believe these things were happening, and we didn't give them too much credence.

A few significant factors began to emerge that may have had something to do with it. My father-in-law happened to have been a presidential advisor all the way from the Truman administration through the Nixon administration. He was instrumental in development of the atomic bomb, and also in research that was going on at Los Alamos, New Mexico. I always was very curious about how he could have been a presidential advisor through so many administrations, and it may have had something to do with UFOs. It was all top-secret stuff, and he never could discuss what he did.

When I got together with his daughter, it seemed like the contacts increased at a tremendous rate. The whole time we were together, which was basically from 1970 to 1975, there were just dozens and dozens of incidents that occurred. I can't explain them. I can't explain why they occurred during that period of time. Things have occurred since my ex-wife and I split up, but not with the intensity that they occurred during the time we were together. My feeling is that my former father-in-law may have been involved in contact or possibly have been an early abductee, and as a result, since these contacts seem to run along family lines, his daughter was also an abductee, along with myself. It may have been that she was the one being abducted and not myself. Maybe I was just "switched off," as is sometimes reported in other cases. I don't know, and that's why I'm very careful about saying that I may or may not have been abducted on occasions, because maybe I was just there and not the object of the abduction.

However, the incidents have occurred on a fairly regular basis even since my ex-wife and I split up. So, it's hard to say whether I was the object or she was the object or we were both objects of abduction during that period of time. I know that I've had experiences that go right up to this year [1990], and I would expect that I would continue to have experiences, based on the frequency with which they've occurred over the years.

ML: Can you reveal the name of your former father-in-law?

T: [long pause] I can't do that without compromising the identity of my former wife, which I'm not willing to do. But I can say this. I believe I've found references to him in some UFO-related documents that refer to a "Dr. Noyes." That would not be a red flag to most people, but he lived on Noyes Drive, and apparently his pseudonym was Noyes. I can't really say much about what he did, but I'm sure that if he was involved in UFO matters, it was not directly under his name. It would have been under a pseudonym, and I think I've figured out what the pseudonym is.

ML: If you had a concentrated series of experiences starting in the early 1970s, I imagine that at least some of these experiences must have been confusing or upsetting to you. How were you affected emotionally and mentally by this?

T: During the height of these experiences, I suffered from anxiety, became easily confused and hypersensitive and went through periods of depression. Many times I was confused as to what was actually happening, and I questioned my ability to perceive reality.

M: Were there certain kinds of experiences that seemed particularly confusing or unreal to you?

T: One example occurred in April of 1970. My wife and I — though we weren't married yet — were visiting our friends Ray and Nancy, who lived in a farmhouse in a heavily wooded area outside of Baltimore. They were kind of hippy-culture people, very nice. We went up there on a number of occasions to visit. On this particular evening, we arrived at about 6:00 or 6:30. Daylight savings had started, so it was staying light until about eight o'clock.

I remember we were talking. I started a sentence, and right in the middle of the sentence, it went from light to dark outside. There wasn't a break in the sentence or anything, but it went from light to pitch black. At the time, I finished my sentence and looked around, and nobody else even seemed to be aware that it had just gone from daylight to pitch black.

ML: Did you say anything about that?

T: I started to, but nobody else seemed to notice it at all. I felt a little stupid saying anything, so I didn't.

ML: Did you have a sense of missing time on that occasion? Did you look at your watch and see that time had passed?

T: I assume there was missing time, but I don't recall looking at my watch.

ML: Did you discuss it with your wife afterwards?

T: No, I never did.

ML: Can you recall anything else about that occurrence besides the fact that it seemingly went from light to dark?

T: The thing that impressed me most of all was that nobody else even seemed to flinch. I started to say something, but I could see that nobody else was even concerned about it. So I thought there was something wrong with me.

ML: Were there other incidents during this period that gave you a similar feeling?

T: I had another experience that on the surface had nothing to do with UFOs at all. However, upon closer examination, it may be UFO-related. I believe it was on November 4, 1972. I was going over San Marcos Pass, just outside of Santa Barbara. What happens up there quite often is that you get fog at the top of the pass. I was on a motorcycle with my wife. As we encountered the fog, I got really terrified about driving on the road because I couldn't see. I had to drive on the reflectors to see where I was on the road. I knew that if a car came over the pass, they wouldn't slow down like I had to, and they wouldn't see me until they hit me. So I decided to turn off at the top of the pass and go back down a side road that went through the Kinevan Ranch.

This ranch had a number of structures on the property, one of which was an old stage stop that was used back in the 1880s. You'd go over a little bridge, and it was off on the right-hand side. Going down this road, which is one lane, I felt fairly safe, because I knew the road and I knew that if there was another vehicle coming, it would have to go very slowly. As I went down across the bridge, I could see that there was a party going on at this particular house. I could see people talking out around the cars, and I could hear music from the house. I could see the windows of the house lit up in the fog. I drove within five or six feet of the people who were standing out by the cars. After that, I went down the road, came out below the fog and went back to Santa Barbara.

The next day I was up in that area, looking to buy some property to build a house, and I drove by the site of the house where I'd seen the party. And to my surprise, it was burned to the ground. There wasn't anything left standing, and it was obvious that a recent fire there had destroyed the house. And I thought, my God, that house must have burned last night. But I didn't think too much more about it until later that afternoon, when I mentioned to a friend that I'd seen a party at this house last night and now all of a sudden it's gone. This was a Sunday afternoon. When I described the house to him in detail — he talked to me quite a bit to make sure we were talking about the same house — he informed me that he knew the house very well, and that it had burned to the ground six weeks before. I thought he was joking, so I went down to the local newspaper the next morning, Monday, and looked up the article. That house *had* burned to the ground about six weeks before. There was a party going on that particular evening, and for some reason the fire department didn't come until it was too late to save the house.[3]

I just thought that something was really wrong. Here I had seen something that had occurred six weeks before, and I had no explanation for it whatsoever. Since then, I have maintained that I somehow entered a time-warp when I entered the fog. I can't explain it. I don't know anybody who can. All I know is that the house did not physically exist at the time I saw it.

ML: Why do you think this experience was UFO-related?

T: For years I didn't make the connection. But this incident occurred in the mountains above Santa Barbara where I've had numerous UFO experiences over the years. I now believe this experience might have masked something else that was going on. I'd like to know what it masked.

There's another reason why that particular vicinity has significance to me. There are lots a very old Chumash Indian cave paintings up there, and they all depict objects in the sky. Some of these paintings date back six hundred years, and some might be over a thousand years old.

ML: What kinds of objects do they depict?

T: If you look at the paintings, you can visualize saucer-type vehicles as well as strange-looking entities. The things that are painted on the ceilings of these caves supposedly depict things that were in the air. To get to some of the best caves, you have to back-pack in. It's worth the effort to go and see them. You can see that they depict some sort of vehicles in the sky. And there were no vehicles in the sky at those times, unless something very unusual was going on. My assumption is that this is an area that's had contact for probably thousands of years.

ML: During this incident in the fog, your wife was with you. Do you believe she saw it just the way you did?

T: Yes. What I'm talking about, in all the events I've referred to here, are situations where there were one or more other witnesses besides myself. I have a feeling that if one person sees something, it could be imagination, hallucination or whatever. But if two people see it, it's doubtful that it's just imagination. There've been a number of incidents where I was by myself, and I choose not to talk about those too much, other than just idle curiosity, because there's no way that they can be verified. In this particular case, my wife was there, and she observed the same thing. She was aware of the conversation I had later on in the afternoon with my friend, and that the house did not physically exist. We both thought this was a little strange, but here again, we did not put a lot of importance on it, whereas looking back, I think it was a very significant event.

ML: How would you say these experiences affected your relationship with your former wife?

T: I'd say they had a negative effect on the relationship, for reasons that I can't really pin down. Just the constant barrage of unexplained experiences put a strain on what was reality and what wasn't. After the marriage, I almost felt as if the whole time we were together wasn't real. Of course, it was; but so many instances happened that couldn't be explained. And I think one of the things that bothers me to this day is that we really made no effort to talk about it. One thing happened right after another, until the point where I developed anxiety and paranoia and everything else. I mean, if every time you turn around, there's another unexplainable event going on, what would you do? How are you supposed to react? You can't explain it to yourself or anybody else. That's basically what happened.

The relationship broke up in July of 1975. I've always considered my former wife to be a very special person, and I still do today. But this was a determining factor in the breakup.

ML: Today, you're a successful professional photographer. Have you ever photographed a UFO?

T: No, I haven't, primarily because all the times I've observed UFOs, I haven't had a camera with me. I know that's very strange, coming from a professional photographer. But if I'm not out to photograph something, many times I don't have a camera with me. In recent years, I've carried a disposable camera in each vehicle that I drive, so that I can photograph anything that occurs. But most of these cases occurred at night, and a camera might not have been much use under those circumstances anyway.

ML: At any time, during any of your encounters or possible abduction experiences, did you see or hear anything that could perhaps help to identify who you were dealing with? What evidence do you have for that?

T: In my childhood experiences, my Whodie could be a typical "gray" type of entity, large head, large almond-shaped eyes, jumpsuit type clothing that was very tight-fitting, long arms, long legs, long fingers. When I see photographs or drawings of the Grays, they look very familiar to me, and I don't know where the familiarity comes from. I have a feeling that I have seen those entities before on a number of occasions.

I think that I've felt a communication on numerous occasions, but it's not words, it's more like feelings. I've tried to duplicate this, but you have to have a willing person to do this with. You transmit your thoughts, but not in words. I'm convinced that the aliens communicate with people through feelings. There's no sentence structure. There's a feeling of something, and that's the communication. That's why the communication can occur in any language. It's beyond language. Every now and then I have things that come into my head and are just there, things that tend to make me go in one direction or another. That's what I mean when I say that they have possibly influenced what I'm doing in my life.

ML: How do you feel about exploring this further for yourself?

T: I think it's important to explore it further. I think something significant has happened in these events over the years. Exactly what, I'm not sure. I think probably hypnotic regression is very useful in discovering these things. I think that the conscious recollection of events is only a partial of what actually occurred. The subconscious is probably the key to many people's experiences. In my case, and I think in a lot of people's cases, it may be necessary to use hypnosis or other means to uncover what actually occurred. I have enough conscious recollections to know that something occurred. I'm fairly certain that I have a number of screen memories that were placed there to block out whatever did occur.

ML: Among those, you might include the party at the house and the owls. Are there others that stand out?

T: Yes, there was one up around a ghost town on the eastern slope of the Sierras. As I was camped in my motor home up in that area, on the side of a road on some BLM land, I had an experience at about 10 o'clock in the evening, when I heard slamming doors. I knew I was the only one around for miles. I could see in both directions, so I knew that nobody else was approaching me. It went on from about 10 o'clock until about 3 o'clock in the morning.
	One thing that made this very significant was that I had my watch next to the bed, and I punched the light on the watch

to see what time it was. Ten o'clock appeared, and then the time just disappeared from the dial on the watch and the light stayed on. It would not go off. There were electrical disturbances that evening in the motor home that I couldn't explain. Everything seemed to be functioning fine the next morning except for the watch. The watch never worked again. I thought the battery was the problem, so I went out and got a new battery for it. When I put the new battery in it, the light came on, but the watch never told time again. I think something fried that watch during that evening.

The next morning, I got up and walked down the road in both directions to see if there were any tracks of anybody who might have come near enough for me to hear them. I walked about a half-mile down the road in one direction, and about a quarter-mile in the other direction. In neither case were there any tire tracks. The only tire tracks I found were my own. It is a remote area where there's not any traffic to speak of. There was no vehicle within a distance that I could hear, especially to slam doors. I don't know what actually made the noise, but I believe this might also be a screen memory of an incident. It wouldn't have occurred to me that that was the case, except for the watch. The watch I still have, and someday I'm going to have somebody take a look at it and try to figure out what caused the watch to completely die on me.[4] The watch was only a couple of months old at the time, so it shouldn't have failed. However, electronic things can fail for other reasons.

ML: In this incident, as I understand it, you neither saw nor heard anything that gave you a specific feeling that this could be a UFO incident. Is that true?

T: No, I didn't see anything, and if I didn't know so much about UFOs and abduction experiences that other people have had, I never would have connected this to a UFO incident. The reason I did was simply because of the electrical malfunction of the watch and the other things in the motor home. Something interrupted the electrical function of the motor home that particular evening. This is a common occurrence with certain types of UFOs that have been reported.

In this area that I was in, I've had a number of experiences since 1974 that could be UFO-related. Some of them were sightings, and others were just happenings that seemed totally out of place. It's an area that is close to some of the military bases that supposedly have operating U.S.-controlled UFOs, near the Nevada-California border. I don't know whether that has anything to do with it or not, but it's an area where there are a lot of UFO sightings. In fact, local residents there have told me of UFOs that have come while they were sitting in a hot springs in the area, and the UFOs have shown a light down on the hot springs while they were in it. The light would stay on for 40 to 60 seconds and then suddenly go out, and they would see this dark object, totally silent, that would just float away. They also reported objects that cross the horizon at tremendous speeds. At that particular hot springs, I myself have seen an object that went from horizon to horizon in just a matter of seconds. So I believe they are telling the truth, since I've seen something similar to what they have described.

ML: What's the most recent such experience that stands out in your mind?

T: Probably the most recent that I can directly attribute to UFO activity was August 23, 1990. I was camped in an area outside of a ghost town, and I was asleep. What happened is that the area where I was camped lit up brighter than daylight. All I could see was white light outside. When I opened the curtains, I saw a streak of white light that went almost straight up, at a slight angle and at a tremendous rate of speed. And being awakened from a light sleep, at first I thought it was a meteor. But then I thought, no, it's going in the wrong direction. I looked at my watch just after this occurred, and it said 4:23. There were three or four other people camped in the area at the time. They were all asleep and did not observe this at all. This is one of the incidents that I'll talk about, but I don't give as much credence to it simply because there was no other witness who could verify what I saw. That doesn't mean it didn't happen. It's just that I feel verification is very important if you're going to give this any credence at all.

ML: Let me invite you to speculate a bit. You've had an unusual number of first-hand experiences, to which you've added considerable study of the UFO phenomenon. What do you think is going on? How do you put it all together and make sense of it for yourself?

T: I believe that we probably have visitations here from other planets or other galaxies. UFOs are probably real -- I don't have any real doubt in my mind about that. However, I'm very cautious about saying that, in the sense that you need to get hard evidence to prove that to people. If somebody hasn't had experiences such as I've had, they would say that I'm full of baloney, and I would expect that from most people. I think it's beyond our comprehension that vehicles can operate in the atmosphere at these incredible speeds and do these incredible "stop on a dime" maneuvers and right-angle turns, things that we would consider virtually impossible. But to put it in perspective, from my understanding, anybody visiting this planet from other planets is probably somewhere between 10,000 and 50,000 years ahead of us in development. That would be like comparing ourselves to a cave-man who comes out and sees what is available in our world today. A cave-man would not understand automobiles, computers, all the things that we take for granted. I think that the possibility of other people visiting here from other places is very high, and I think that their technology is so far beyond ours that many of the things we say are unexplainable may be everyday occurrences to them.

I think, personally, that there is some validity to the concept that they are abducting people on a fairly regular basis. They probably are doing some genetic engineering of the human species, along with their own. I think that there is a feeling among those who are visiting that they would like to see the earth not be completely destroyed by our own actions, through pollution and environmental destruction. That's sort of far-fetched for a lot of people, but the activities that I've become involved in are basically toward preservation of the environment. I would like to think, as I said earlier, that those are all my ideas, but I also think there's a possibility that my ideas have been manipulated or directed toward that type of goal, through my involvement over the years with these beings.

The encounters that I've had have not been of the scary type. Seeing something that's unexplainable is kind of scary at times, but I've never really felt that I was in any physical danger. I have a strong feeling that there has been some communication that may have directed what I'm doing in my life, as a result of my encounters. There's no evidence of that, so I can't really say that it's true, but that's my feeling.

ML: Some people who regard themselves as abductees seem to have very negative feelings about their experiences, but you sound as if you have mixed or somewhat positive feelings.

T: I think that a lot of people tend to fear the unknown. In my case, I'm curious about the unknown, and I pursue answers. I've never had any real fear of the encounters that I've had. I think there has been some communication to me that there's no need to fear, and I've taken that as being truthful. Many of the places where I do my work are remote locations where UFO activity does occur. I've never thought of the UFO activity as being related to those choices, but it may well be. So, my feeling is not negative at all. At times, I've expected I would have negative feelings from all this, since so many other people have reported negative things — but in my case it's been positive.

ML: That may be encouraging to some people. It may well be that we're not dealing here with anything that's hostile or negative. It's certainly mysterious, and you've made that very clear. Is there anything else that you'd like to comment on before we conclude?

T: I think that there is a lot more going on than the general public is aware of, and I hope that the aliens' presence here will soon be known, so that people can utilize this important information to assist the human race in its development, rather than go through this shroud of secrecy and mystery. I think that the mystery of this whole subject is something that leads to anxiety for a lot of people, and I think that the most positive direction would be for people to be made aware of the fact that we have had contact with people from other worlds. And if we haven't, then I think that's important to bring out as well. I think that there should be some effort to verify this, because there are a lot of people who are probably suffering over whether or not this is actually going on. It would be great if it could be verified one way or the other.

I do expect that most people who read this might not believe much of what I've said, in the sense that if they haven't had a personal experience, they would say this is just imagination. But I think that those who have had such experiences know exactly what I'm talking about. I think it's important that these people not feel that there's something wrong with them. Maybe they are the chosen ones, and everybody else is not. It can be a very positive thing for everybody, if people can look at it in a positive light.

Donald M. Ware

Chapter Six
Donald M. Ware:
The "Larger Reality" Behind UFOs

Donald M. Ware is a retired Air Force Lt. Colonel. During his
26 years in the U.S. military, he served as a jet fighter pilot and
earned a Masters Degree in nuclear engineering. An eyewitness to the famous UFO overflights of Washington, DC in the
summer of 1952, Don has studied the UFO phenomenon all his
adult life. Today, he is Eastern Regional Director for the Mutual
UFO Network, coordinating MUFON activities in eighteen
states, a post he assumed after serving six years as MUFON
State Director in his home state of Florida. He played a key role
in MUFON's extensive investigation of the Gulf Breeze, Florida
UFO sightings, concluding that the alleged UFO photos taken
by Gulf Breeze resident Ed Walters and others in 1987-88 are
authentic.

I first met Don on August 12, 1990, when he invited me to
interview him at his home in Ft. Walton Beach. My main objective at the outset was to record his story of the Gulf Breeze
investigation. However, I discovered that Don wished to address
a wide range of other matters. It is no exaggeration to say that
I was stunned by our conversation, during which Don revealed
his belief that alien beings are orchestrating the total transformation of the human species and preparing to usher in a new
historical epoch on the earth. All this, he says, is part of a "larger
reality" that is being revealed to humanity at this time. — ML

Don Ware: Let me give you a little background to get this
started. I was sixteen years old, heading home one evening in
Arlington, Virginia. It was 11:30 at night, and I looked up and
saw seven star-like objects in somewhat random motion over
Washington, DC. I stood there and watched them very intently

for about ten minutes, because I remembered reading the headlines in the newspaper the previous Sunday morning.[1] This was 26 July, 1952. The next morning, sure enough, huge headlines — around the world, I was told — that there were a number of UFOs up there, being seen by hundreds of people on the ground, being reported by many airline pilots, on three radar sets simultaneously, and chased by Air Force interceptors. That was the second Saturday night in a row that this had happened. The guys at Project Bluebook didn't even find out about it until the next morning when they read the news, which tells you what Bluebook's position was in those days.

I'm now convinced that the reason this occurred was so it *would* be in the headlines. The guys in the UFOs were *trying* to make headlines, in my opinion.

ML: Are you willing to go any further with your opinion on what their motives are? If they want to make their presence known, what else would you say about their intentions?

DW: Look at history. If you go back and accept the Roswell incident as being valid, which I do; and if you accept the stories of a meeting between Eisenhower and some alien beings, a demonstration given to him at Edwards Air Force Base shortly after he took office,[2] which sounds plausible to me at the present time — there's less evidence for that, but there apparently were six witnesses and some have been talking — it indicates that a long time ago there was interaction between higher intelligences and some human beings. These seem to me to be government interactions. I think there was such interaction near Bentwaters Air Base in England in 1980, and also probably in 1968 at Holloman Air Force Base.

If you've seen "UFOs: It Has Begun," the rewrite of "UFOs: Past, Present and Future,"[3] I think that was an early effort by somebody in the government to get valid information concerning the larger reality that UFOs are part of into public view. We know that back in 1938, the public got really uptight about alien beings.[4] If, in fact, our government learned, sometime in the late 1940s and early '50s, or maybe even later, that there is another species here that is developing a hybrid with us, and that this hybrid will eventually be the dominant inhabitant of this planet, that is a pretty scary idea to some people. Without having a deeper understanding of the larger reality, you can see how that would be a frightening idea. And it takes time to change the thinking of large numbers of people.

Consider, for example, a letter from "the friendly spook" to [UFO researcher and author] Wendelle Stevens, dated late February, 1989. The "spook" said a number of times that our government has tested the waters to see what the public would do if told what was really going on. Apparently, back in the late 1940's, they ran several tests to determine whether or not the President should make an announcement over national radio. The "spook" said that the reaction was overwhelmingly negative. Ninety-seven percent of the people took one of two positions. One was to shoot first and ask questions later, and the other was to look at UFOs as representing the devil, which would have a negative influence on religions, in the view of those who were assessing the situation.

Probably as early as 1949, which is the date of the contingency plan listed as "Attachment G" of the MJ-12 Briefing Document our government had decided to educate us slowly and may even have had some timetable for when we needed to know certain things. Jaime Shandera told me that there was one U.S. intelligence operative on the set in the making of *The Day the Earth Stood Still* in 1950, and two on the set in the making of *Close Encounters of the Third Kind,* to make those movies rather close to reality. I think our government decided to educate us about the larger reality primarily through fiction, in an effort to keep from scaring us too much. And I think that's still going on. I think when you watch *Star Trek: The Next Generation* on television, or when you watch *Alien Nation,* you are getting concepts put before you that you need to understand if you're going to be able to accept the larger reality.

ML: It sounds as if you consider the government's actions to be essentially benign, perhaps a well-intentioned effort to manage a potential threat while psychologically preparing the public for the truth. Is that a fair statement?

DW: Yes, I think the government actions are managing the threat. Of course, you've got to realize that there are branches of our government that have no idea what other branches of our government are doing. So the waters get muddied a little bit there, of necessity.

Once those in our government who knew what was going on had managed to handle it themselves, I think they recognized that it was necessary to have a long, carefully thought-out program for educating the public. And I think a lot of what we see on TV right now concerning higher intelligences or other dimensions are ideas probably planted by somebody in our government. I know that the way Hollywood works, it's easy to plant those ideas. If it's a good idea, they'll put it on and not ask questions about the source. I know this sounds ridiculous, but right now our five-year-olds are getting almost daily doses of good guys and bad guys popping in and out of various dimensions, or guys of various mutations called teen-age mutant ninja turtles. These are concepts that tend to blow the minds of most people, but concepts you've got to understand if you're going to be able to accept the larger reality that I think is out there and starting to interact with us. There *are* good guys and bad guys of various dimensions and various mutations involved.

Jaime Shandera tells me that he thinks the reason intelligence operatives are interacting with him and have been since late 1982 is that they want him to help cultivate various media personnel for the responsible reporting of government strategies on UFOs.

Here's something that's rather suspicious in my mind. In 1983, Ted Koppel incorporated the company that he used to make his "State of the World" message on December 26, 1988. That program was framed as a message to the aliens. Ted Koppel had picked well-known media personnel, highly thought-of people, to make their statements in that format. So, here you've got some of the most respected people in this country in a one-hour TV special, broadcast in the format of a state-of-the-world message to the aliens.[5] This is the kind of thing that I think our government is behind somehow — I'm sure not directly, but through people like Shandera. And of course, there's talk going around that Bob Lazar may have been used without his knowledge. In other words, somebody in our government wanted the story that he's telling to come out.

I'm absolutely convinced that our government does want certain pieces of information to come out. We UFO investigators have been bugging the government for many years to tell us what they know. We know they know a lot. They're trying to tell us what they know, but they're not going to do it outright. It's going to come through the back door, because nobody in our government can afford to face the press on the issues. If they did come outright with it, they wouldn't be able to perform their normal duties, they'd be harrassed so much for more information. And they have good reasons why they can't tell it all. They have to be in control of what comes out when. Otherwise, it could have some adverse impact.

ML: You speak of the larger reality. I'd like to know what you mean by that.

DW: The larger reality is the basis of all the major religions of the world, and all the secret societies. It's knowledge that was so heavy that only a few could comprehend it, and not thoroughly at that. The larger reality is coming through to us in many different ways now, most of them telepathically. I think the clearest description that I've read in the last couple of years is in the four books of the *Law of One*, which are the transcripts of 104 question-and-answer sessions that Don Elkins had with an entity called Ra between 1981 and 1983.[6]

Don Elkins was, I think, a very interesting fellow. He had a pretty good scientific background, saw his first UFO in 1948 while in pilot training, then became an Eastern Airlines pilot.

By 1955, he had a great deal of time to spend investigating UFOs. By 1962, he was convinced that our scientific community was incapable of providing the answers to questions that his UFO study had caused him to have. For example, how do these guys walk through walls? We know they do it, and it blows the mind of any conventional scientist.

Don decided that if he were going to learn the answers, he was going to have to adopt some alternative means of investigation. He experimented with a lot of alternative means and decided that the telepathic vocal process was the most scientifically acceptable way of getting information. This process has been called trance channeling. I think he considered this an acceptable approach because he could pick the people, the time, the place, the questions; he could record the event in audio or video; and he could repeat the experiments independently in different places around the world and compare results. That's very close to the scientific procedure. By 1981, he'd been investigating UFOs and the larger reality that they represent for nineteen years, when he and his group in Louisville, Kentucky, made contact with an entity who called himself Ra. Don's group at that time included Carla Rueckert as the channel, himself as the questioner and Jim McCarty as the back-up person in the room.

Ra said he was the same individual who had influenced the Egyptian civilization for thousands of years. He said he was a "sixth density being." He said it was impossible to describe the larger reality because of language limitations, but he would do his best to answer any question that Don posed concerning the larger reality or human history, as long as it didn't affect living persons. I think Don asked a lot of the right questions, and I think the answers are supported, apparently independently, by different people around the world.

Ra describes the human experience as being "third density existence." He says that we have a soul that does not die when we die, and that at some later point it reincarnates in another human form. He says we go through a number of different incarnations, trying to learn certain lessons. But primarily, the reason for the human experience is to determine through our own free will whether we will orient ourselves toward service to others or service to self, which is described as positive or negative polarization. That's what human existence is all about: polarization either toward the positive or negative, service to others or service to self.

Ra says there's no such thing as good and bad — you have to have positive and negative or nothing happens. The soul will not evolve unless you've got the selfish folks down here amongst us. They are the catalysts that cause us to make choices, hundreds of choices every day that contribute toward our orientation, toward our spiritual growth throughout many incarnations.

Ra says that at some point there will be a transformation on this planet, where the "fourth density positive existence" will exist here rather than the human existence. He says the main reason for fourth density existence is to develop unconditional love. But to do this, we need greatly improved telepathic ability over what we now have, and — he doesn't say this, but he insinuates it — that would be too tough to do unless the negatively oriented individuals were separated out from the positively oriented individuals, and went through their own fourth density evolution on a different planet. He says the Earth is destined to be a fourth density positive planet at some point in the future, after the transformation.

When Ra was asked how to determine who is harvestable — he used that word, "harvestable" — that is, who is sufficiently oriented toward service to others to enter that new society on this planet, he said that 50% orientation toward service to others is about as good a position as he could give any of us. If you're more than 95% oriented toward service to self, you're considered harvestable in the negative, and you will end up in some future incarnation on a planet up in the Orion group. He says only about a fifth, or maybe a billion human beings on this planet, will be harvestable. Probably the majority of the people on this planet haven't gone through enough incarnations to be sufficiently oriented one way or the other, and after they die, their souls will reincarnate in some other human-like form on some other planet.

Ra says that this planet, this whole solar system, is moving into a section of the galaxy where the magnetic fields are different. They will interact with the core of our planet to cause a slight heating, which will cause an increase in volcanic activity, and with it some plate shifting and tectonic changes. It will be a period of increased opportunity for people to make choices. In other words, toward a certain phase of this transformation period, there will be a lot of activity going on, and I think we may be seeing the start of that now. My gut feeling is that this transformation period is perhaps a hundred years in length, of which we're near the mid-point already.

Ra says, getting back to further steps in the evolution of our soul, that once we have mastered unconditional love, we graduate to fifth density existence, and there we develop true wisdom. Once we graduate from that into sixth density experience, we become as he is, which he describes as a "social memory complex," a conglomeration of many, many souls. He describes us as a mind-body-spirit complex, indicating that we do have a mind, a body, and a spirit which is eternal. He says that he went through his human-like existence on our planet Venus, 2.6 billion years ago. He says as this planet moves into the section of the galaxy where the magnetic fields are different, the basic vibratory level will change. Now, I don't know whether he's talking about the 7.8 hertz [the so-called Shuman Resonance — ed.] that people say is the natural vibration level of this planet or not, but as that changes somewhat, it makes life more compatible with fourth density existence than it does with third density human-like existence.

Ra says there's another level above his, which presumably he knows less about, but in that level of existence, seventh density, both positive and negative spirits combine into one, essentially for the glory of God, I guess. But he says that throughout fourth, fifth and sixth density, there are both positive and negative influences, and their home planets are different. It's only in the third density existence that you have positive and negative beings living together on the same planet.

ML: You seem to think that there's a direct connection between this idea of a larger reality and the UFO activity on this planet. Could you be specific about that?

DW: I think that this description I've been giving you is something that was made evident to some high-level members of our government over thirty years ago. I think somebody in our government has been interacting with higher intelligences for at least thirty-some years.

ML: Are you saying, for example, that the beings we typically call the Grays are actually here on a spiritual mission?

DW: We have been told that a species from another planet has been given permission, by some intergalactic governmental agency, to develop a form which will be suitable for the reincarnation of our souls and theirs, a form compatible with our biosphere that will be used for fourth density positive experience on this planet at some point in the future. This may be what Jesus was referring to when he talked about heaven on earth — that the negatively oriented and the selfish people were separated out, because living here with positively oriented people would be too tough to do if you could read the minds of your spouse and your children, as you presumably would be able to do. The species that is apparently being developed, from the descriptions given to us by many abductees, appears to have perhaps 35% greater brain capacity, increased telepathic ability, and stands maybe a foot shorter than we do. Those are the three characteristics that seem fairly evident at this point.

ML: Are you now speaking as Don Ware, spiritual seeker? What's the connection between what you're saying and your position at MUFON?

DW: I'm speaking now as Don Ware, seeker of the truth. My current position with MUFON is as Eastern Regional Director, and MUFON is dedicated to the scientific investigation of UFOs. I think we can better direct our scientific investigation of UFOs if we start to acquire some appreciation of the larger reality from which they come.

ML: I've had the impression that MUFON is rather conservative in the matters that you're addressing.

DW: MUFON *is* rather conservative in the matters that I'm addressing, but a number of members of MUFON are not so closed-minded that they haven't expanded their reading into deeper subjects concerning the larger reality.

ML: Would you say that the so-called transition to fourth density corresponds in any way to Jacques Vallee's notion about there being an interdimensional aspect to the UFO phenomenon?

DW: Yes. In fact, I'm quite impressed. When I read *Fellowship* by Brad Steiger, and *Dimensions* by Jacques Vallee,[7] recognizing that Vallee comes from a more scientific perspective and Steiger from a more spiritual perspective, I see in those two books that both of them are heading in the same direction. And I think that where they're heading is close to the truth. I recommend reading those two books back to back.

ML: I see on your bookshelf a copy of Trevor Constable's book, *The Cosmic Pulse of Life.*[8] I haven't met many people in the UFO field who are aware of this particular book. But Trevor Constable quite some time ago proposed that some of the beings we might call aliens are actually indigenous to the earth and are part of an etheric level of existence. He even claims to have photographed such beings using infrared film, and some Italian researchers say they have duplicated his results. Constable agrees with Jacques Vallee's idea that the extraterrestrial hypothesis is inadequate to explain what we're really dealing with here. What's your view on that?

DW: I think that most hypotheses that people come up with are in part correct. They perhaps lack accuracy because of ignorance of the larger picture. I've been to four UFO symposiums so far this year, and at those symposiums you meet a lot of New Age types. I've seen albums full of beautiful pictures of people surrounded by their auras, for example. This is the kind of thing that Trevor Constable talks about. It appears that there is some energy that is associated with our bodies that is not flesh and blood as we would recognize it, but is sometimes observed as an aura that continues to exist after our bodies die. If these energies — etheric bodies, mental bodies or whatever they are — actually exist, then maybe some exist in our atmosphere. I don't know. They've got to be somewhere.

ML: There are many investigators who feel that the activity of the so-called Grays does not have the appearance of a benign intent. How can you account for the negative aspects of abduction, for example, in terms of the larger reality?

DW: I don't like to use the term "Grays," because I think you're trying to put a species-label upon a form that we don't know enough about yet. You know, a lot of us can't even tell Japanese from Chinese. There are differences. I think that there are a number of different species interacting with us. Some seem to be positively oriented, some seem to be negatively oriented. I think we are being interacted with by beings of different levels of existence, or different densities or dimensions. In one respect, the devil is still out there trying to steal our souls, trying to encourage us to make decisions that are selfish in nature.

ML: And some of what we might call the alien presence could have that aspect?

DW: The preponderance of the evidence that I have seen concerning the abduction phenomenon indicates that the purpose is to develop this hybrid species, compatible with the biosphere of this planet, that is necessary to house our souls in some future incarnation. I'm convinced that there are very large numbers of these little hybrid guys out there somewhere, and that tells me that the time is near when these guys will be on this planet en masse. I suspect that there are hybrids in underground bases, hybrids in bases beneath the sea, perhaps in large vehicles in orbit, perhaps on Mars or the moon or wherever. This is just supposition. But we have government intelligence operatives telling us that six million Americans have been on board UFOs, whether they know it or not. That's one in forty.

ML: Government intelligence operatives have told you this?

DW: The same person who gave [UFO researcher and author] Timothy Good his copy of the MJ-12 documents told him that: one in forty. Allen Hynek mentioned that before he died: one in forty had been on board UFOs. Budd Hopkins, two years ago when I asked him, said that extrapolation from the number of letters that he and Whitley Strieber had been receiving from their books indicated again that the number of abductees has got to be at least one million. So, we're talking about a lot of people that have been aboard UFOs. And the primary reason for most of the abductions, as I see it, is the hybridization process. They're developing these little guys. A number of abductees evidently have also been involved in some kind of an emotional transfer process with the little guys, and I think this has got to be toward the latter stages of the project.

There's evidence that there has been genetic manipulation of Homo sapiens a number of times in the past. I've heard that the species that has been given permission to develop the hybrid, using their own genes combined with ours, is from the fourth planet of the Zeta Reticuli star system. There is some suspicion that there is at least one other planet in Zeta Reticuli that does have higher intelligence on it. This planet is becoming unsuitable for continued fourth density existence. And that's why they were picked, because they need a planet that their souls can migrate to. In other words, they would like to have a planet in which there will be a form that will be compatible to accept their souls in some future incarnation also. So it appears to me that we human beings in some future incarnation will reincarnate in a new species living on this planet, along with souls of Zeta Reticulans, if we are positively oriented. This is, of course, all highly speculative. But once you start getting this input from more than three different sources, I feel free to at least talk about it. I don't put a lot of it in writing until I get quite a bit of verification for it, but these are things I've gotten from what appear to be at least three independent sources.

ML: Many people no doubt regard the whole alien question as inherently threatening. You obviously regard it as very important, but not necessarily threatening, even if it means the end of human life as we know it. How did you come to your present viewpoint?

DW: Personally, it took me two years of investigating UFOs, after I saw those things in 1952, to decide in my own mind that some UFOs are vehicles controlled by more advanced intelligence. It took me another ten years to figure out that somebody in our government has known that for a fact at least since 1947. When I retired from the Air Force in early 1983 and had time to expand in my reading, I read a number of books on the ancient astronaut subject and became impressed with the work of Zecharia Sitchin.[9] Shortly thereafter, I decided that somebody has been watching us for a very long time.

Certain things happened in early 1989 that caused me to become more spiritually oriented in my reading. I had already started to read things on the religions. I've had a great interest in all the world's mysteries ever since I can remember. And I'd studied very basic data on the world's great mysteries and religions, and saw a lot of similarities between religious teachings in different parts of the world. I just had a feeling that there was a connection between UFOs and religion, because almost every religion has got some kind of flying disk. The gods of old are associated with flying disks. I decided there had to be a connection between UFOs and religion, but I never could figure out what it was until about the first of 1989, when I decided in my own mind that both the UFO phenomenon and religions are avenues through which we get a glimpse of a much larger reality.

As soon as I made that connection, before I had started publicizing it, some interesting things started happening. First of all, a lady called me on the phone and said, "I need to talk to you face to face." She lived about three hundred miles away, and this was a Sunday evening. I said I could see her on Wednesday, and she said OK. She came, and she told me that she wanted to give me a message. She said that there was something concerning nuclear weaponry going on at Eglin Air Force Base Reservation [located adjacent to Fort Walton Beach, FL — ed.] that upset some folks with whom she was in telepathic communication, something that concerned them considerably. They had told her it was like playing Russian roulette. She gave me a book she had written, which I found very interesting, and then left.

I asked myself, "Should I do anything about this message? Why did she drive three hundred miles? Why did she feel compelled to give me this message? Was there a reason?" I discussed this with two of my retired military friends, and they thought I ought to do something about it. So we discussed what I could do, and I decided I would pass the message on to somebody at the base. I picked the general who had the greatest technical education, called his secretary and said I wanted to talk to him. She said, "He's got an opening next Tuesday morning." This was Thursday afternoon. I said, "Well, I'm getting ready to leave town. It's going to have to be this afternoon or tomorrow, or we'll have to forget about it." She said, "What do you want to talk to him about?" I said, "I want to give him some information from an unusual source." She said, "OK, I'll squeeze you in between his staff meetings tomorrow morning." I went down there and sure enough, the general came out of his staff meeting, went into his office and said I could go in. I had prepared my statement first in written form. I gave him the circumstances under which I had received the message, then gave him the message. He looked at me square in the eye and said, "I don't know everything that's going on in this reservation. But I know who does, and I will make sure he gets the message." I thought that was a very reasonable response.

Since then, I have received over a dozen communications that apparently come from higher intelligences who mention my name. These came through five different individuals using three different telepathic sources. And they're starting to get my attention. I've never received any telepathic communications myself. I suspect the reason is that, if I did, it would reduce my credibility among my peers. Anybody who hears voices or receives telepathic information is looked upon as being a little crazy by some folks. But I think I can talk about these communications, which are received through other people and given to me because my name was mentioned, without greatly reducing my credibility.

ML: Do you know if anything has ever been done with the Eglin information?

DW: No. I've learned through my study the last couple of years that almost everyone who is contacted through these telepathic communications is tested in one way or another, and I suspect that my acting upon telepathically acquired information was a test. Because of that, I've been receiving all these other communications.

ML: You've said there's evidently a connection between UFOs and religion. That brings to mind the recent incident involving six AWOL soldiers, five men and one woman, who were picked up in Gulf Breeze.[10] Reportedly, these soldiers went AWOL in

Germany and came to Florida expecting a spiritual event of some sort involving UFOs. I've heard it suggested that this event was more important than most people realize. What's your perspective on this?

DW: Well, let's look at those six people. They range in age from 19 to 26. They all got at least a high school degree, then enlisted in the army and were probably among the more intelligent folk to be put through code school in Pensacola. I expect that most young military folk in their indoctrination are told that the Commies are the bad guys and you really have to watch out, because they'll stick it to you if you let them. These guys get sent over to Europe on their first tour, and they see things happening there very rapidly, things they really weren't prepared for in their army indoctrination. They see the Berlin Wall crumble, they see Communism disappear in the buffer countries and even having trouble in Russia. Evidently, these guys were attuned to religious or New Age philosophies, possibly fundamentalist philosophy concerning rapture and second coming. There is evidence that at least one of them was acquainted with a well-known psychic in the Pensacola area, and one of them claimed to be receiving telepathic information from some apparent higher intelligence. Given this, I can see where events might have occurred that would cause these young folks to not feel that the consequences of leaving their place of duty was so important in relation to what else was going on in the world, particularly at a time when our army in Europe was being drawn down considerably and was looking for ways to give people an early out.

It was the day after the Pensacola MUFON symposium was officially over, July 9 [1990], that these folks showed up in the Gulf Breeze-Pensacola area. It was well known that there was a lot of media hype associated with that symposium. I don't know why they came there. But after they were picked up, a number of statements were made by acquaintances in the U.S., friends in Europe and military folks at the Pentagon concerning the religious orientation of their actions, and these guys were very quickly let out of the service. Immediately [after their discharge], at least some of them came back to Gulf Breeze.

As I see it, the primary result of what happened is that several words showed up on front pages of newspapers around the country several times over the next week or two. Those words were rapture, second coming, and anti-Christ. Now, I recognize that our government is not allowed to address religious issues according to the Constitution, but if our government or somebody in our government felt it was time the American people started at least thinking about those issues, how would they do it? There is a possibility in my mind that the leader of that group may have been in cahoots with somebody in our intelligence service to get the media, which they knew was in Gulf Breeze, to pick up on those three subjects. I expect it didn't happen the way it might have been planned, if that was the scenario. But I don't see any necessity for the other fellows with him to have any knowledge whatsoever of the real reason why they went to Gulf Breeze. That's one possible scenario as to why that happened.

ML: Would you say there is any parallel between your idea of a transition to fourth density existence and what some would call the rapture or the second coming?

DW: I suspect that various concepts of the rapture are somewhat distorted. Most religious teachings are distorted as time goes on. When you talk about the rapture, you're talking about the mechanics of how something might happen. And I really don't trust all the details of how that might work. I think there's a lot of room for misinterpretation.

But I do see a lot of people being taken up in UFOs right now. For example, there's the story of Bill Herman up in Charleston, South Carolina, published by Wendelle Stevens under the title *UFO Contact From Reticulum*. Bill was abducted in 1978 and again in 1979. In the meantime, Frederick Valentich was picked up in his little plane with a UFO hovering over him, and he disappeared over the Bass Strait in Australia.[11] Bill Herman asked the aliens what happened to Fred Valentich and was told he chose not to return. Now, whether that kind of thing can be associated with what some people describe as the rapture, I don't know.

I also see that when you look at various aspects of human society, you see a lot of asymptotic curves. You see things happening in a manner that can't continue to happen. Something drastically different has got to happen, which gives more credence in my mind that we are near the transformation time.

One of the books that I've read in the last few months is *The Watchers* by Ray Fowler, a new book that follows up Fowler's two previous books about the multiple abductions of Betty Andreasson.[12] We know that many abductees are given information that they are told they will not remember until the time is right. Betty Andreasson was recently told, "Now is the time." And she was told and shown a number of very interesting things that she was meant to pass on to Ray Fowler, for him to pass on to you and me. That's what *The Watchers* is about. It describes through Betty Andreasson the larger reality that you can read about, for example, in *The Law of One*.

If this planet is in fact going to be the home for a future species that is generally a foot shorter, has 35% greater brain capacity and greater telepathic ability, where people can learn to develop unconditional love — if this is going to be heaven on earth as described by Jesus — then someone up there may be interested in us not destroying the earth ecologically. Someone up there may be interested in us not having a massive nuclear exchange, not polluting our waters, not cutting down every tree on the face of the earth.

ML: I've heard speculation from several researchers that what's recently occurred in U.S.-Soviet relations, and the drastic changes in Eastern Europe, are in some way alien-related. That sounds like it fits your idea.

DW: Would you turn off your tape recorder?

[Don did not wish to be on record with the following story. I summarize it from notes:

Don said that he had heard from a source he considers reliable that Mikhail Gorbachev was visited in 1985 by two "beings" during a meeting with his top advisors. These beings, describing themselves as Ascended Masters, informed Gorbachev that it was his and the Soviets' responsibility to initiate an immediate end to the threat of nuclear war. The beings stated that they could enforce this demand, and in order that Gorbachev would not underestimate their seriousness, they told him that there would soon be a major nuclear accident at Chernobyl.

Despite trusting his source, Don said he found this story unbelievable until he recalled the numerous warnings against nuclear war given to UFO contactees of the 1950s, as well as a statement from Ra that the nuclear fireball destroys souls.

After Don finished this story, the tape recording was resumed. — ML]

ML: What can you say about the allegations that humans and aliens are working together on various projects, perhaps in underground bases?

DW: I think that the two-hour television documentary, "UFO Cover-up: Live!" on October 14, 1988 involved some cooperation with U.S. intelligence operatives. On that program, "Falcon" said that some alien species had operational control of at least part of Area 51, which is a pretty phenomenal statement. He also said that the vehicle witnessed by Betty Cash and Vickie Landrum on 29 December, 1980 in Texas was an alien vehicle being piloted by U.S. Air Force pilots, another phenomenal statement.

I think we have had a serious R&D program, probably based in Nevada, concerning alien technology for thirty or forty years. I am fully aware that our government can keep a secret when they really want to. I understand there are at least four different stealth vehicles in operation at the present time:

214 UFOs and the Alien Presence

the F-19, F-117A, the Aurora and the B-2. Two of them, the Aurora and the F-19, we know very little about.

ML: The Air Force denies that the Aurora even exists.

DW: And I think they deny that the F-19 exists. I know a lot of people who have worked in Area 51. I know a lot of people who have encountered UFOs while testing our fastest aircraft. I've been told that our astronauts have seen UFOs on a number of occasions, that more often than not when we send up a space shuttle, it has company. These stories I accept. I get them over and over again from credible people. Bob Lazar's story also appears basically feasible to me right now.

I've been told and have recognized in the past that any time the government releases information to us, there is usually some disinformation associated with it. That is for the purpose of allowing our intelligence community to raise or lower public reaction to that information as they see fit. That concept sounds feasible to me. I think that happens.

ML: Some military sources have said that they think we might one day have to fight the aliens. The gist of your remarks suggests to me that you think the government is essentially willing to go along with whatever the aliens have in mind. What do you think about this concept of fighting the aliens?

DW: I think it's hogwash. I have seen no information indicating that we're going to have to fight the aliens. I do recognize that each of us on an individual level may interact with higher intelligences at one time or another, both positive and negative. I recognize that there is such a thing as psychic attack from negatively oriented higher intelligences. In that respect, I can accept the idea of fighting the aliens.

ML: But in terms of physical conflict with high energy weapons, you think not?

DW: I haven't seen enough evidence so far to indicate that SDI has any purpose other than that which has been publicized. I may be wrong, but I haven't seen the evidence. I know that when we first designed SDI, it was extremely important that we do something to prevent our adversaries from thinking they could get away with a first strike, to make sure that nuclear weapons were not launched upon us whether from the Soviet Union or from Third World countries that were rapidly developing them. That sounded like a reasonable program to me. I support SDI. I don't think it has anything to do with aliens.

ML: The Gulf Breeze UFO sightings have achieved a unique prominence in American ufology during the past few years. Some researchers regard this case as proof positive that UFOs are intentionally interacting with humans, while others see it as a state-of-the-art hoax. During 1990, a serious debunking campaign was mounted against the main witness, Ed Walters. What's your view on the latest developments in this case?

DW: In regard to the debunking, the evidence I've seen indicates that the UFO model Ed was accused of using in his photos was apparently made from materials taken from his trash shortly after the 7th of September, 1989, well after he had moved out of that house. The accusation of fraud did receive a lot of media attention and has swayed the thinking of some folks. It has also had several other results. It has caused an increase in the sale of his book, which I think is generally good, because I think his photos are the next best thing to seeing a UFO. Most people will not believe that UFOs are real until they see one for themselves. I think the reason that Ed had 18 photographic opportunities in five and a half months was so that he could get some good pictures that people would see. I think that was the purpose for which the aliens posed for Ed. And enough other people were allowed to see them in the process to support his case, to make it extremely difficult for the debunkers to discredit it in the mind of the world.

The statements of Tommy Smith are a bit more mysterious. But I was aware very early in the sequence of events that some teenager had some pictures of UFOs that he wouldn't show to anybody. The reason he wouldn't show them, I think, is because he was greatly concerned about his parents' reaction to them becoming public, and him being associated with them. We were at that time investigating pictures provided by Believer Bill, by Jane, a little bit later by Mike Johnson and several others. Some, of course, turned out to be street lights, airplanes, videotapes out of focus and that kind of thing. We were really busy. We had seven people working on it pretty hard. So we didn't think a whole lot about this other individual, Tommy Smith, whose name Ed would not tell us at that time, because Tommy didn't want him to. Ed is a man of great integrity and great concern, particularly as regards young people.

I don't know why Tommy Smith made the statements he did. I have a transcript and I see a number of inaccuracies in his statements, which leads me to suspect that some of the other accusations he made are inaccurate. He accused [Ed's son] Danny Walters of collaborating in a hoax. Danny Walters has stated that that's not true — his statement was published in the *Gulf Breeze Sentinel*. Tommy accused Hank Boland of collaborating in a hoax. Hank Boland's lengthy statement to the contrary was published in the *Gulf Breeze Sentinel*. Dr. Bruce Maccabee, who did the technical analysis of Ed's photos, was brought to town by *Unsolved Mysteries* recently to look at the six photographs that were provided by Tommy Smith. Dr. Maccabee says they look like real UFOs to him. This is what we were told earlier. There is a young fellow named Rob who says that he saw the photos that Tommy Smith had very early on, probably before Ed's photos ever came out in the newspaper. Rob was led to believe that these were real UFO photographs that Tommy Smith had taken, and that Tommy Smith was scared to death about his father's reaction. Apparently he had tested his father's reaction and it was not good, and he had refused to go public with them.

ML: Do the six photographs that were in Tommy Smith's possession show a UFO similar to Ed Walters' UFO?

DW: They do. They look like the Gulf Breeze Type 1 vehicle.

ML: Is it your supposition that Tommy Smith took those photographs himself?

DW: That's what Rob says, and that's what Ed says Tommy told him.

ML: The Center for UFO Studies has declared the Gulf Breeze case to be an outright fraud. As you understand it, what is their rationale for taking such a negative view?

DW: I can't answer that question. However, I can tell you that at least twice during the Gulf Breeze photographic session period, I called [CUFOS president and scientific director] Mark Rodeghier. I got his answering machine and left him the message that evidently the people in CUFOS didn't know what was going on in Gulf Breeze. I suggested that before they published further information about Gulf Breeze, they ought to talk to someone who's down here investigating it. I told Mark that I was available any time. I got no response. CUFOS printed a lot of things that weren't true. They were writing things that they knew nothing about. I don't know what other people think, but CUFOS lost a lot of credibility in my mind as a result of Gulf Breeze.

ML: And yet the Gulf Breeze situation seems to have put a division in MUFON too, as a result of the debunking. Is that true?

DW: One member of our board of directors resigned recently, apparently as a result of that. There are a number of people who will not agree on what this UFO phenomenon is all about, and if they let their disagreement hinder their ability to do the job, which is seeking the truth, let them work with whatever organization they want to work with.

ML: Following the Pensacola MUFON conference [July 1990], Linda Howe told me that she sees a fairly dramatic shift in the overall tone of UFO research. Can you summarize your sense of what's occurring today in American ufology?

DW: As time goes on, people are recognizing that reality is much more extensive than our scientific community has given it credit for. UFO investigators, who are open to a lot of borderline science, are becoming more knowledgeable in certain esoteric areas that the general scientific community ignores. I was told by a nuclear physics professor in 1968 that the most difficult decision any scientist has to make is his choice of reading material, and I think that is absolutely true. Consequently, I have been encouraging UFO investigators to read things that will expand their view of the larger reality, and other UFO investigators in MUFON have been doing the same thing. I think that's one reason those people who have the time to do a great deal of reading are getting a broader picture and are willing to accept the idea that the UFO phenomenon is giving us a glimpse of something much larger.

Conclusion

Stanton Friedman, nuclear physicist, relates the story of two seasoned Air Force pilots who try unsuccessfully to close on a UFO in broad daylight, communicating all the while with a ground controller who watches the entire episode through binoculars. Friedman's voice rises a notch as he concludes, taking on a tone that seems to acknowledge the absurdity of his tale. "What do you do with a case like that?" he asks. "You can't say they're lying. What for? This was a classified report. It makes no sense."

Next to some of the accounts in this book, the alleged episode over George Air Force Base is downright mundane. Yet, it is the very profusion of such "mundane" cases that provides foundation for the more extraordinary claims of alien encounter. No doubt, some people — perhaps some readers of this book — will feel inclined to reject even the Roswell incident as inherently unacceptable, for to do otherwise opens a Pandora's Box of disorienting possibilities. To anyone who has experienced mixed feelings during the reading of this book, I can only say that I sympathize.

There is no way at present to determine how much of the foregoing testimony is true, or what it actually means. All of the speakers have plainly acknowledged their own moments of doubt and turmoil in the face of the phenomena they have come to know so well. All of them remain seekers of an elusive truth, a truth they regard as exceedingly important.

They surely do not agree with one another on every point. Bob Lazar, for example, says he tends only to believe what his eyes have seen — but then, he says he's seen things that most people, including some UFO researchers, automatically dismiss as ridiculous. Don Ware and Budd Hopkins agree on the outlandish notion that aliens are engineering a hybrid species on this planet; yet, Hopkins senses impending disaster, while Ware expects spiritual transformation. Linda Howe thinks that

some of what she knows is too upsetting to divulge publicly —
and thus she finds herself uncomfortably close to supporting
the cover-up which she and all UFO researchers deplore.

The official cover-up is, for that matter, probably the one
issue about which nearly all UFO researchers agree. As impossible as it may seem on first inspection, governments *can* keep
such huge and long-running secrets when they must, as explained by both Stanton Friedman and Don Ware. Why our
government has felt the need for such secrecy is not entirely
clear, though ample justification is suggested by Friedman and
Ware, as well as Linda Howe and Budd Hopkins. Despite all
efforts, however, it may be that the cover-up cannot be maintained much longer. What happens next is anybody's guess.

Assuming that alien beings are present on the earth, there
is no agreement among researchers as to their nature or motives. The diversity of evidence on these issues lends itself best,
perhaps, to the interpretation that a veritable menagerie of
non-human intelligent beings is present among us, doing all
manner of strange or marvelous things. The behavior of some,
notably the so-called Grays, seems unpleasant by most accounts. Yet, Tom feels that his encounters, though mysterious,
have had a good effect in his life. Even Budd Hopkins, who sees
mainly trauma resulting from close encounters, cannot see
willful malice in alien behavior. It is as if "alien behavior"
remains inscrutable from an objective point of view, being
strictly "in the eye of the beholder."

All such speculation is pointless, of course, if the basic
claims of an alien presence are untrue. The professional debunkers would simply have us agree that the speakers in this
book and others like them are crazy, deluded or consciously
fraudulent. Then, all will be well — we can get back to "reality."
But if this book is not just a compendium of crazed delusions,
then we are challenged to consider, as Don Ware suggests, that
a "larger reality" than we have ever imagined is coming into
focus before our eyes.

It is safe to assume that the speakers in this book are not
crazy. On the contrary, they are all basically healthy and well-

adjusted. They are capable and accomplished in their respective fields. None of them claims to possess any final truth, all of them acknowledge the apparent absurdities in their data, yet they all willingly accept the risks inherent in speaking about what they have learned. Their commitment to grapple with the evidence and speak aloud their uncomfortable thoughts may be, as Gregory Bateson said, "the difference that makes the difference" in the unfolding human-alien drama.

Every reader of this book is invited to follow their lead. It is not important to agree or to believe. It is important to grapple with the evidence, and to give voice to your questions, upsets, insights and discoveries. To do so is to brave an emerging new world, in which long-cherished assumptions fall apart and breathtaking discoveries await only our willingness to see. Will you engage in this stupendous quest? The choice is yours.

Michael Lindemann

Footnotes

Chapter One: Stanton Friedman

1. Philip J. Klass is the former senior editor for the magazine *Aviation Week and Space Technology*. He is also the preeminent UFO debunker in America. His books include *UFOs: the Public Deceived* (Random House, 1968), *UFOs Explained* (Random House, 1974) and *UFO-Abductions: A Dangerous Game* (Prometheus Books, 1988). Howard Blum, in his book *Out There* (Simon and Schuster, 1990), ably describes how Klass became the darling of UFO skeptics (p. 214ff) and his intellectual battle with Stanton Friedman, Bill Moore and others over the authenticity of the MJ-12 documents (p.243ff).

2. Ted R. Phillips, *Physical Traces Associated With UFO Sightings*, published by the Center for UFO Studies, Chicago, 1975. Currently out of print.

3. Some researchers are convinced that the U.S. government is building aircraft considerably more exotic than those mentioned by Friedman, possibly including so-called "alien replicated vehicles" or ARVs. For example, see William F. Hamilton's *Cosmic Top Secret*, p.80ff (Inner Light Publications, 1991) See also *Aviation Week & Space Technology* magazine, October 1, 1990, p.20f, and December 24, 1990, p.41f, for discussion of super-secret, allegedly hypersonic aircraft now flying out of Edwards Air Force Base and Groom Lake, Nevada.

4. George Air Force Base is located just south of Victorville, California. The sighting in question took place on May 9, 1952 at about 11:15 PDT. Pilots in two F-86 fighters, along with three control tower personnel and another pilot on the ground, kept the disk-shaped object in view for over ten minutes. This sighting became Project Bluebook case #1194 and was listed as unidentified.

5. In 1966, with mounting pressure from Congress and the general public, the U.S. Air Force commissioned the University of Colorado to undertake a special study of UFOs under the direction of Dr. Edward Condon. The resulting report, *Scientific Study of Unidentified Flying Objects*, was published in 1969. The so-called Condon Report has since become notorious as an intentional whitewash of UFO evidence. Nonetheless, the body of the report contains a great deal of provocative data that was not acknowledged in subsequent summaries. Condon himself, along with agents of the CIA and other sources with whom he worked, evidently believed that a book

giving credence to claims of alien activity was not in the national interest. One person close to the investigation reported Condon as saying that "he had given the matter much thought, and had decided that if the answer was to be a positive finding of ETH [extraterrestrial hypothesis], he would not make the finding public, but would take the report, in his briefcase, to the President's Science Advisor, and have the decision made in Washington." See Timothy Good, *Above Top Secret* (William Morrow, 1988) p.345-6.

6. A 1988 Pulitzer Prize went to journalist Tim Weiner for his three-part series of articles on the Pentagon's "black budget" spending, published February 8, 9 and 10, 1987, in the *Philadelphia Inquirer*. Weiner published a book in 1990 based on these articles, titled *Blank Check* (Warner Books, New York).

7. The top-secret memorandum was sent by Wilbert B. Smith to officials in the Canadian government. The memo reads, in part: "I made discrete inquiries through the Canadian Embassy staff in Washington who were able to obtain for me the following information: a) The matter is the most highly classified subject in the United States Government, rating higher even than the H-bomb. b) Flying saucers exist. c) Their modus operandi is unknown but concentrated effort is being made by a small group headed by Doctor Vannevar Bush. d) The entire matter is considered by the United States authorities to be of tremendous significance." (Good, *Above Top Secret*, p.183)

8. See *The Search for the Manchurian Candidate* by John Marks, Bantam Books, 1978.

9. Public interest in flying saucers reached fever pitch following the widely-reported sighting of nine disk-shaped objects over the Cascade Mountains in Washington state by pilot Kenneth Arnold on June 24, 1947. The term "flying saucer" was coined by the press to describe what Arnold saw. A classified FBI memorandum of the time credited Arnold's report as highly reliable. During the same period, many other sightings were also reported by military and civilian pilots.

10. *The Roswell Incident*, by Charles Berlitz and William L. Moore (G.P. Putnam's Sons, 1980)

11. USAF Project Grudge/Bluebook reports 1-12 were declassified in September, 1960 and published as a 235-page special report by NICAP (National Investigations Committee on Aerial Phenomena) in 1968. Grudge/Bluebook Report 13 was never released to the public.

12. Milton William (Bill) Cooper first came to the attention of UFO researchers in December, 1988, when he filed a report on the CompuServe and ParaNet computer bulletin boards, purporting to divulge secret government information on UFOs that he had learned while serving in the Navy in 1972. His highly controversial views are explained in his book, *Behold a Pale Horse*, Light Technology Publishing, 1991.

There seems little doubt that a secret Project Sign was undertaken by the U.S. Air Force, probably in 1947, as one of several related efforts to learn more about UFOs. According to the MJ-12 document, "SIGN evolved into Project GRUDGE in December of 1948. The operation is currently [November 1952] being conducted under the code name BLUE BOOK."

13. In September of 1947, General Nathan Twining was head of Air Materiel Command and General George Schulgen headed the Air Intelligence Requirements Division at the Pentagon. Twining's memo was in response to a request from Air Intelligence concerning "flying disks." Twining stated, in part: "The phenomenon reported is something real and not visionary or fictitious....There are objects probably approximating the shape of a disk, of such appreciable size as to appear to be as large as man-made aircraft....The reported operating characteristics such as extreme rates of climb, maneuverability...and action which must be considered *evasive* when sighted or contacted by friendly aircraft and radar, lend belief to the possibility that some of the objects are controlled either manually, automatically or remotely." (see Good, *Above Top Secret*, p.260f)

14. Bill Moore described his dealings with government agents and UFO researcher Paul Bennewitz in a speech at the MUFON conference in Las Vegas on July 1, 1989. The full text of Moore's speech was printed in his "Focus" newsletter, volume 4, issues 4-6, dated June 30, 1989 and available from the Fair Witness Project, 4219 W. Olive Ave. Suite 247, Burbank, CA 91505.

15. The two-hour television production "UFO Cover-Up: Live!" was broadcast nationwide on October 14, 1988. Prominently featured were two alleged government agents code-named "Condor" and "Falcon," whose faces and voices were electronically altered.

16. *UFO Abductions: The Measure of the Mystery*, in two volumes, by Thomas E. Bullard (1987), an analysis of 270 cases, published by and available from the Fund for UFO Research, P.O. Box 277, Mt. Rainier, MD 20712.

17. Best-selling author Whitley Strieber described his alleged encounters with alien beings in *Communion: A True Story* (Morrow/Beech Tree Books,

1987) and its sequel, *Transformation: The Breakthrough* (Morrow/Beech Tree Books, 1988). A thorough analysis of Strieber's case was presented by journalist Ed Conroy in *Report on Communion* (Morrow, 1989).

18. Arguments for and against the debunking claims can be found in the *Pensacola News Journal* of June 10 and June 17, 1990; and in the *Gulf Breeze Sentinel* of June 21, 1990.

Chapter Two: Linda Moulton Howe

1. The September 30, 1974 issue of *Newsweek* magazine reported the animal mutilation phenomenon then sweeping the Great Plains states in an article titled "Mysteries: The Midnight Marauder." The article notes that "a helicopter often has been seen hovering over the range around the time of a mutilation," giving rise to speculation that marijuana smugglers or cattle rustlers might be the mutilators. Also sharing the blame were "devotees of witchcraft" and "strange creatures resembling bears and gorillas," while "at least one farmer claims that a shiny UFO landed in a field where a slaughtered animal was later found."

2. The complete transcript of Dr. Leo Sprinkle's regressive hypnosis session with Judy Doraty on March 13, 1980 was published in *An Alien Harvest* by Linda Moulton Howe (Linda Moulton Howe Productions, 1989), p.301ff.

3. Subsequent to her interview, Linda said that she had recently heard from another abductee that the "reptilian" species works for a species of gray that is coming to be known as the "praying mantis" type. She also said that she now distinguishes two broad types of grays. The "praying mantis" type has many insect-like characteristics: large, hairless head tapering to a very narrow chin; very large "wrap-around" eyes; body and appendages dispro-portionately long and slender by human standards. A second type, which she calls the "eben," has a broader face with mongoloid-like features and is generally rounder and more full-bodied. She believes the "eben" type is very ancient and very advanced, both mentally and spiritually. Both types, she said, seem to have benign intentions toward humans.

   Other alleged abductees have recently told researchers in California that at least one type of gray seems "enslaved" by the "reptilian" species. Credible eyewitness reports of the "reptilians" were more numerous in 1990 than in prior years, and tended to indicate non-benign intentions toward humans. Often a connection between the reptilians and the grays was mentioned; but various reports contradict each other on the apparent nature of this connection.

4. Travis Walton told his own story in *The Walton Experience: The Incredible Account of One Man's Abduction by a UFO* (Berkley Medallion Books, 1978)

5. *Situation Red: The UFO Siege*, by Leonard Stringfield (Fawcett Crest Books, 1977). Stringfield has also published several compilations of evidence on alleged UFO crash/retrievals, including *The UFO Crash/Retrieval Syndrome, Status Report II* (38 pages) and *UFO Crash/Retrievals: Amassing the Evidence, Status Report III* (53 pages), both available from MUFON, 103 Oldtowne Road, Seguin, TX 78155-4099.

6. Vice-President Quayle, who is also Chairman of the National Space Council, spoke before the American Institute of Aeronautics and Astronautics on May 1, 1990, endorsing their call for an international effort to hunt down and destroy asteroids headed for the earth. The Institute distributed an official position paper on the subject on May 14, and newspapers ran the story on May 15, 1990.

7. John Judge was interviewed August 12, 1989 on the Los Angeles radio station KPFK on the subject of UFOs, which he describes as "Unidentified Fascist Observatories." Most legitimate UFO sightings, he says, are "actually sightings of an advanced but hidden technology controlled by the United States government and developed under the auspices of the advanced aerospace and munitions rocket work done in Nazi Germany at the end of the war as part of Hitler's push to develop ultimate weapons." Judge seems able to spot fascists behind every tree, but he's not alone in pointing out a possible Nazi connection to UFOs of terrestrial origin. See, for example, *Genesis* by W. A. Harbinson (Dell Publishing, 1980), a history-based novel that describes Nazi efforts under Gestapo chief Heinrich Himmler to develop a saucer-shaped, jet-propelled aircraft. See also *Intercept UFO* by Renato Vesco (Zebra Publications, 1974). It is a matter of record that both the U.S. and Soviet space programs benefited greatly from former Nazi rocket scientists who were given safe haven, and classified jobs, in the two countries. What they actually knew and imparted to their new hosts about saucer-type aircraft is a closely guarded secret.

Chapter Three: Bob Lazar

1. *UFO* magazine, vol 5, number 6 (Nov/Dec, 1990) p. 19

2. Lazar was the first person to reveal that alleged flight-tests of alien craft could be viewed with impunity — though some fifteen miles away — from a desolate stretch of BLM land along State Highway 375 near the Nevada Nuclear Test Site. The area known as Mailbox Road, at mile-mark 29-1/2 on

route 375, has since become perhaps the world's favorite haunt of would-be saucer watchers.

3. "The Billy Goodman Happening," a late-night talk show on Las Vegas radio station KVEG, regularly featured Bob Lazar and other UFO experts until host Goodman was suddenly bumped from the air. Irate listeners claimed Goodman must be cutting too close to the truth, since his high ratings argued against other explanations for his dismissal. Goodman was later reinstated by the station.

Chapter Four: Budd Hopkins

1. "Sane Citizen Sees UFO in New Jersey," by Budd Hopkins, in *Village Voice*, March 1, 1976, p.12

2. *Missing Time: A Documented Study of UFO Abductions*, Richard Marek Publishers, New York, 1981

3. *The Search for the Manchurian Candidate*, by John Marks, Bantam Books, 1979; and "The Controllers: A New Hypothesis of Alien Abductions," by Martin Cannon (draft version September 1989)

4. The dictionary definition of confabulation is "familiar talk; chat; prattle." In research using hypnosis, the term is used to connote the tendency of witnesses to inadvertently combine memories of real experience with information gained from other sources, including the imagination.

5. This conference was held as planned. One significant outcome was that a philanthropist, who wishes to remain anonymous, offered to fund a nationwide survey of abduction experiences in America. This survey, to be undertaken during the summer of 1991, will be the most ambitious independently-funded UFO research project in history.

6. Dr. David M. Jacobs is Associate Professor of History at Temple University, author of *The UFO Controversy in America* (Indiana University Press, 1975) and member of the board of directors of the Intruders Foundation.

7. *Intruders: The Incredible Visitations at Copley Woods*, Random House, 1987

8. *The Gods of Eden*, by William Bramley, Dahlin Family Press, San Jose, 1990

9. During 1990, "crop circles" in Great Britain became so elaborate that researchers took to calling them by other names, such as "agriglyphs." Some

researchers also began noting the possibility that these formations could have literal meanings. Some symbols in the grain fields look exactly like pictographs from various ancient cultures, including Norse and Sumerian. No one has yet [May 1991] claimed a precise translation, but crypto-zoologist Jon Erik Beckjord, among others, believes such translations could come soon. Among several possibilities Beckjord is examining: the crop formations mark points of special interest to the aliens, or serve as warnings from one alien group to another, or are meant to initiate communication with humans.

10. *International UFO Reporter*, September/October 1987, published by the Center for UFO Studies, 2457 W. Peterson Avenue, Chicago, IL 60659

11. Dr. Leo Sprinkle of the University of Wyoming was one of the first psychologists to take a professional interest in UFOs and abduction claims. He has worked with hundreds of alleged abductees and believes he too was abducted as a child. More often than not, his cases reveal a seemingly benign intent on the part of the aliens.

Chapter Five: Tom

1. Santa Barbara is located on a south-facing coastline. The Santa Barbara Channel runs east-west between the coast and the Channel Islands. Directly south of Santa Barbara is Santa Cruz Island, the largest of the Channel Islands. Its near shore is approximately 24 miles from the Santa Barbara coast. Thus, the UFOs described in this sighting were evidently at least 24 miles from Tom's vantage point. If, as claimed, they went behind the island so as to back-light it, they would have been at least 30 miles away.

2. Evidently Tom means the "gray" type of entity depicted by Whitley Strieber and others. He clarifies this point later in the interview.

3. The local daily newspaper, the *Santa Barbara News-Press*, reported the total destruction of this house by fire on September 13, 1972. Cause of the fire was not determined. Two young women, students at the nearby university, were staying in the house on the night of the fire. They had invited two young men to join them and had entertained themselves playing records late into the evening. Ranch owner Loisgene Kinevan remembers seeing that "every light in the house" was on that night. Miss Kinevan made the first call to the nearby Forest Service fire department after hearing screams at about 3 am, but inexplicably, the fire department did not respond until almost half an hour later. By that time, the house was a total loss.

4. On January 3, 1991, Tom met with a very experienced researcher in northern California and told him about the watch. This researcher, who wishes to remain anonymous, said he would make inquiries concerning analysis of the watch. Shortly thereafter, he discussed the matter with a man employed by a major aerospace company. The man was sympathetic to the problem posed by the watch. His advice, however, was unexpected: "Have it examined by a reputable psychic." The researcher ascertained that the man was entirely serious. As this book goes to press, no further steps have been taken.

Chapter Six: Donald Ware

1. Washington-area papers may have headlined the July 19 sightings, but other papers did not. The *New York Times, Los Angeles Times* and *London Times* didn't run the story at all. Granted, news competition was stiff that weekend. The Olympics opened in Helsinki on July 19. On July 21, the fractious Democratic Party convention opened in Chicago, and the biggest U.S. earthquake since 1906 rocked Los Angeles. But when UFOs buzzed DC again on July 26, the story played everywhere – even though Adlai Stevenson had just been drafted to head the Democratic ticket, Bob Mathias had just set a world record in the decathlon, and a huge aftershock had just hit Los Angeles. Page one, *New York Times*, July 28: "'Objects' Outstrip Jets Over Capital. Spotted Second Time in Week by Radar, but Interceptors Fail to Make Contact." Page one, *Los Angeles Times*, July 28 (6-column headline): "Jets Chase Sky Objects Over Capital. Mysterious Craft, Spotted by Radar, Elude Pursuers." *London Times*, July 29: "Aerial Objects Over Washington."

2. In February of 1954, President Eisenhower briefly disappeared from a Palm Springs golfing vacation. The press went into an uproar — the New York AP wire even flashed speculation that Ike had died — until Press Secretary James Haggerty belatedly announced that the president had been taken to the dentist. In the aftermath of this odd incident, many felt the dentist story was a cover-up. One rumor has it that Eisenhower actually was taken to nearby Edwards Air Force Base, where he witnessed a number of alien craft on the ground and perhaps met living aliens. This story was told in a letter from one Gerald Light, an alleged eye-witness, to Meade Layne, then-director of Borderland Sciences Research Foundation. The letter and commentary can be found in *The Roswell Incident* by Charles Berlitz and William L. Moore (Berkley paperback edition, 1988; p.129ff).

3. *UFOs: Past, Present and Future* by Robert Emenegger, Ballantine Books, New York, 1974

4. Probably a reference to Orson Welles' 1938 Halloween radio broadcast, *War of the Worlds*, which caused pandemonium because thousands of listeners thought the theatrics were real.

5. Ted Koppel's one-hour special, "News From Earth," was broadcast on the ABC television network December 26, 1988.

6. *The Law of One*, in four volumes, published by and available from Light/Lines Research, P.O. Box 5195, Louisville, KY 40205. The first volume has also been published as *The Ra Material*, Whitford Press, 1984.

7. *The Fellowship: Spiritual Contact Between Humans and Outer Space Beings*, by Brad Steiger, Ballantine Books (pbk ed.) 1989; and *Dimensions: A Casebook of Alien Contact*, by Jacques Vallee, Contemporary Books, 1988

8. *The Cosmic Pulse of Life*, by Trevor James Constable, (revised edition), Borderland Sciences Research Foundation, 1990

9. Zecharia Sitchin, an expert on the culture of ancient Sumeria, has written a series of provocative books collectively called *The Earth Chronicles*, in which he argues that the Sumerian civilization was far too advanced, particularly in astronomy, to have achieved their knowledge on their own. They were taught, Sitchin says, by humanoid beings from a hidden planet in our own solar system, the same "planet X" postulated by modern astronomers. Furthermore, he says, ancient religious texts, including the Bible, allude to these "super-beings" again and again. The most recent of Sitchin's books is the first to make direct reference to UFO activity on earth and summarizes the argument put forth in previous volumes. See *Genesis Revisited*, Avon Books, New York, 1990.

10. The story was reported in papers nationwide, emphasizing that the six U.S. soldiers who deserted their post in Germany were evidently associated with an "End of the World" cult and thought they were on a mission to "destroy the Anti-Christ." See, for example, the *Los Angeles Times* of July 18 and July 20, 1990.

11. The Valentich story is recounted in *Melbourne Episode* by Richard F. Haines, L.D.S. Press, Los Altos, CA, 1987.

12. *The Watchers: The Secret Design Behind UFO Abduction*, by Raymond E. Fowler, Bantam Books, 1990. This book recapitulates and updates Fowler's earlier books, *The Andreasson Affair* and *The Andreasson Affair, Phase Two*.

Bibliography

Berlitz, Charles, and Moore, William L.: *The Roswell Incident,* G.P. Putnam's Sons, 1980

Blum, Howard: *Out There,* Simon and Schuster, 1990

Bramley, William: *The Gods of Eden,* Dahlin Family Press, San Jose, 1990

Bullard, Thomas E.: *UFO Abductions: The Measure of the Mystery,* in two volumes, published by and available from the Fund for UFO Research, P.O. Box 277, Mt. Rainier, MD 20712; 1987

Conroy, Ed: *Report on Communion,* William Morrow, 1989

Constable, Trevor James:*The Cosmic Pulse of Life,* (revised edition), Borderland Sciences Research Foundation, 1990

Cooper, Milton William: *Behold a Pale Horse,* Light Technology Publishing, 1991

Elders, Lee J. et all: *UFO...Contact from the Pleiades, Vol I* (revised), Genesis III Publishing, Phoenix, 1980

Elkins, Don et al: *The Law of One,* in four volumes, published by and available from Light/Lines Research, P.O. Box 5195, Louisville, KY 40205. The first volume has also been published as *The Ra Material,* Whitford Press, 1984

Emenegger, Robert:*UFOs: Past, Present and Future* , Ballantine Books, New York, 1974

Fowler, Raymond E.: *The Watchers: The Secret Design Behind UFO Abduction,* Bantam Books, 1990

Good, Timothy: *Above Top Secret: The Worldwide UFO Cover-up*, William Morrow, 1988

Haines, Richard F.: *Melbourne Episode* , L.D.S. Press, Los Altos, CA, 1987

Hamilton, William F.: *Cosmic Top Secret*, Inner Light Publications, 1991

Hickson, Charles and Mendez, William: *UFO Contact at Pascagoula*, published by and available from Charles Hickson, 2024 Carol Drive, Gautier, MS 39553; 1983

Hopkins, Budd: *Intruders: The Incredible Visitations at Copley Woods*, Random House, 1987

_____: *Missing Time: A Documented Study of UFO Abductions*, Richard Marek Publishers, New York, 1981

Howe, Linda Moulton: *An Alien Harvest*, published by and available from Linda Moulton Howe Productions, P.O. Box 538, Huntingdon Valley, PA 19006-0538; 1989

Jacobs, David: *The UFO Controversy in America*, Indiana University Press, 1975

Kinder, Gary: *Light Years*, Atlantic Monthly Press, 1987

Lindemann, Michael: *UFOs and the Alien Presence: Time for the Truth*, published by and available from the 2020 Group, 3463 State Street, Suite 264, Santa Barbara, CA 93105; 1990

Phillips, Ted R.: *Physical Traces Associated with UFO Sightings*, Center for UFO Studies, Chicago, 1975 (out of print)

Sitchin, Zecharia: *Genesis Revisited*, Avon Books, New York, 1990

Steiger, Brad:*The Fellowship: Spiritual Contact Between Humans and Outer Space Beings*, Ballantine Books (pbk ed.) 1989

Strieber, Whitley: *Communion: A True Story*, Morrow/Beech Tree Books, 1987

_____: *Transformation: The Breakthrough*, Morrow/Beech Tree Books, 1988

Stringfield, Leonard: *Situation Red: The UFO Siege*, Fawcett Crest Books, 1977

_____: *UFO Crash/Retrieval Syndrome, Status Report II*; and *UFO Crash/Retrievals: Amassing the Evidence, Status Report III*; both available from MUFON, 103 Oldtowne Road, Seguin, TX 78155-4099

Vallee, Jacques: *Confrontations: A Scientist's Search for Alien Contact*, Ballantine Books, 1990

_____: *Dimensions: A Casebook of Alien Contact*, Contemporary Books, Chicago, 1988

Walters, Ed and Frances: *The Gulf Breeze Sightings*, William Morrow, 1990

Walton, Travis: *The Walton Experience: The Incredible Account of One Man's Abduction by a UFO*, Berkley Medallion Books, 1978

NOW AVAILABLE
From the 2020 Group

"UFOs and the Alien Presence"
VIDEOTAPE